Mrs Pamela Dudley.
47 Iris Crescent
Bexleyheath
Kent.

Mrs Pamela Dudley.
47 Iris Crescent
Bexleyheath

# PLAYTHEMES ROUND THE YEAR

# PLAYTHEMES ROUND THE YEAR

## for children at home, school and playgroup

## Irene Cockroft

Mills & Boon Limited
London Toronto Sydney

First published in Great Britain 1975 by Mills & Boon Limited,
17–19 Foley Street, London W1A 1DR.

© Irene Cockroft 1975

ISBN 0 263 05611 2

Printed and bound in Great Britain by
Morrison & Gibb Ltd., London and Edinburgh

# Contents

## DEDICATION

Dedicated to all who care for children, with special thanks to Joan Bryant and Barbara Horn of Mills & Boon Ltd for their faith and enthusiasm, to my husband, David, who gave technical advice, and to our children, Abigail and Jonathan, who provided constant inspiration.

## ACKNOWLEDGEMENTS

For permission to use copyright material I am indebted to the following authors, literary executors and publishers:

Evans Brothers Limited for 'In the Mirror' by Elizabeth Fleming, 'The Holiday Train' by Irene Thompson, 'An Eskimo Baby' by Lucy Diamond, 'Pudding Charms' by Charlotte Druitt Cole, and 'Mincemeat' by Elizabeth Gould, from THE BOOK OF A THOUSAND POEMS; Kenneth Stobbs and 'To-morrow's World' (BBC TV) for the centigrade rhyme; The Oxford University Press and Ian Seraillier for 'The Tickle Rhyme' from TALE OF THE MONSTER HORSE; Family Circle magazine for details of how to make a child's counting picture; the Literary Executors of the late Rose Fyleman for 'Man in the Moon', 'Clouds', and 'The Goblin'; Duckworth and Company Limited for 'The Elephant' by Hilaire Belloc from THE BAD CHILD'S BOOK OF BEASTS; A. & C. Black for 'The Postman' from SPEECH RHYMES by Clive Sansom; The Bodley Head for 'Jack Frost' by Gabriel Setoun from A CHILD WORLD; George G. Harrap and Company Limited for 'Aeroplanes' from MUSIC FOR THE NURSERY SCHOOL by Linda Chesterman.

Other verses in this book are either by the author, out of copyright, or traditional. In a few cases it has proved impossible to ascertain the source of rhymes and trace the owners of copyright. I apologise to any owners whose copyright has been unwittingly infringed.

# Introduction

PLAYTHEMES ROUND THE YEAR is a collection of simple play ideas suitable for children from 3 years old upwards, at home, at playgroup, or at primary school. It includes creative activities, nature notes, seasons and festivals, folk-lore, and lots of things that are just fun. Its purpose is to familiarise young children through play with things that will provide a sound foundation for formal learning later.

## HOW TO USE
## PLAYTHEMES ROUND THE YEAR

Use PLAYTHEMES ROUND THE YEAR as you would a calendar, turning over a page at the end of each week. Four weeks have been allowed for every month of the year. Don't try to do everything suggested. Choose those activities best suited to your facilities and the stage of development of your children. Use the index to look up specific activities to fit in with themes of your own choice.

PLAYTHEMES ROUND THE YEAR is intended as a source of inspiration to delve into and adapt rather than as a set course to be followed. Allow plenty of scope for free play and don't expect all the children to join in what you are doing. Some are natural observers rather than doers. Use suggestions and discoveries made by the children to expand your theme. Be ready to drop preconceived plans if something more exciting arises spontaneously during a session. If the children seem tired or if you feel 'under the weather', fall back on familiar activities that do not require much effort. If you find that one of the themes holds the children's interest for longer than a week, by all means explore the subject for as long as interest continues.

You will find some poems and activities adapted to more than one theme in this book. You might think of some rhymes and poems that seem more appropriate than the ones given for certain weeks. This is as it should be. In practice you will probably arrive at a nucleus of a dozen or so rhymes, poems, songs and activities that the children love best and that cannot be repeated too often.

## NOTES ON WORKING WITH
## PRE-SCHOOL PLAYGROUPS

There is no mystique about working with under-fives. They are the offspring of ordinary people. If you are a natural, pleasant, interested person, you are a perfect model for them. Kindliness and common sense will see you through most situations. Should you wish to gain more insight into the psychology of play, there is a list of titles for further reading and a list of useful general reference books at the back of this book.

### Caution! Genius at work

Before you descend, full of well-meaning enthusiasm, on a child who is absorbed in solitary water play, or a shy child who is venturing to join in a group activity, THINK! Might your approach put them off? Of course, it is important to show interest in what the children are doing and to sit and discuss things with them when you can. But always allow the children time for personal, private, silent exploration and discovery before intervening.

### Creative activities

Don't lose sight of your real objective. It is not to produce recognisable pictures or models that please adults. It is to create a desire in the child to experiment with materials to find out what they do, and what he can do with them. Creative activities should spark off new ideas, provide an outlet for emotions, and help to develop skills.

Try to steer a middle course between doing too much for the child, so that his own artistic efforts seem inferior by comparison, and doing too little to help and encourage him, so that he gives up in frustration.

In 'Things for adults to make' you will find more elaborate creations that you can make as gifts for children.

### Story telling

Begin with a positive attention-getter, like showing the children some topical object, or lead in with a well-loved action rhyme. Tell some of your story or poem from memory if you can, and dramatise a little. Personalise by using the names of children in your group whenever it is appropriate.

Many of the books referred to week by week may be found on the shelves of your local library. (Inquire about a quota of tickets for your group.) You might not always be able to find the books referred to, or you might prefer others when you see what is available. Suggestions are made merely to give you an idea of the wealth of lively and appropriate material being published.

## Group activities

A group is made up of individuals. Interest one or two children in an activity, and the others will soon want to join in if it is interesting enough.

## The colour table

It is worth setting aside a table for colour displays. Announce a colour choice for each month and invite the children to contribute objects of that colour that can be spared from home. A colour table serves many purposes:

1 It provides a link with home.
2 When a child chooses something from home to bring for the colour table he is exercising observation and judgement of what is suitable.
3 It shows the value of group effort.
4 When a collection of objects have colour in common, other differences become more apparent, for example size, texture and shape. When the child registers these things, he is laying the foundations of comparison and measurement.

## Sand and water play, large equipment

Although they are not often mentioned in this book, basic play materials like sand and water should be available to the children most of the time if possible, particularly in summer.

A climbing frame and slippery slide provide exciting and satisfying sensations, if you can spare the money and space. Swings and see-saws demand constant adult supervision.

## Music

It would be impossible to find one song book which included most well loved nursery rhymes. It would be impracticable for you to hunt down and buy a long list of books each containing only a few songs for very young children.

A short list of good value, generally available tune books is given at the back of this book. Such a source could not be found for all the songs mentioned in PLAYTHEMES. However, most of them are traditional and there is a good chance that at least one mother in every playgroup will be able to recall them. Otherwise where words are given you could make up simple tunes to suit.

## Safety

Put yourself in the shoes of a mother about to part with her vulnerable 3-year-old for the first time. Stand at the door of your playgroup room and look around. Is the scene reassuring? Or do you see children toddling unsteadily about with pointed scissors, heavy objects propped up uncertainly, unguarded radiators, matches left within reach, chairs stacked against fire doors, dirty lavatories, cups not properly washed, tea towels and hand towels not as clean as they should be, broken, dangerous playthings, doors and gates left open for children to wander onto the road. . . .

Do all the mothers on rota duty know where the first-aid box is kept? Is it out of reach of the children? Is there a pamphlet on first aid to help mothers deal with emergencies? Could a mother in the group organise a talk on first aid by an expert? Do all the mothers know how to open the fire doors? Do they know the correct fire procedure? Could somebody in the group organise a talk by the local fire brigade?

Is the telephone number of the local ambulance service handy? Do you have an arrangement with the nearest doctor for emergency help and do all the helpers know the surgery address? Are there always at least two adults present?

Having said all this, let me add that playgroup emergencies happily seem to be few and far between. This is a credit to the vigilance and responsible attitude of playgroup people in general. Keep up the good work by making sure that you have eliminated every foreseeable risk, and that you are prepared for anything unforeseen.

## Mother-helpers

New mothers have to learn what happens at playgroup just as much as children do. They are bound to feel mystified and inhibited at the start. WHAT'S HAPPENING has been designed to give mothers a better understanding of what their children are doing at playgroup, and more confidence as helpers.

Planning activities with the supervisor can be impossible, because there is always at least one's own child present and children demand a great deal of attention. Before your helping day is due, look up PLAYTHEMES for that week. There may be an activity that you could manage well. Check with the supervisor and if it fits in with her plans, initial that activity in pencil in the playgroup copy of PLAYTHEMES ROUND THE YEAR so that the other helpers will know it is in hand. Make a note if you would like people to save any junk material required, so that the right things are available at the right time.

## TEACHERS

It is hoped that this collection of calendar events and related activities will prove a useful standby and source of inspiration in infant classrooms.

You may find it equally helpful in teaching immigrant children of all ages, for many have to 'begin at the beginning' with a new language and new environment.

You could enrich the material given by adding examples of folk-lore from other countries.

# Some Basic Materials

### SCISSORS

Good quality handicraft scissors with rounded ends.

### PAINT POTS

Plastic liquid detergent containers with inverted tops make spill-proof paint pots.

Powdered poster paints can be thickened with wallpaper paste, flour, or for covering print, with undiluted liquid detergent.

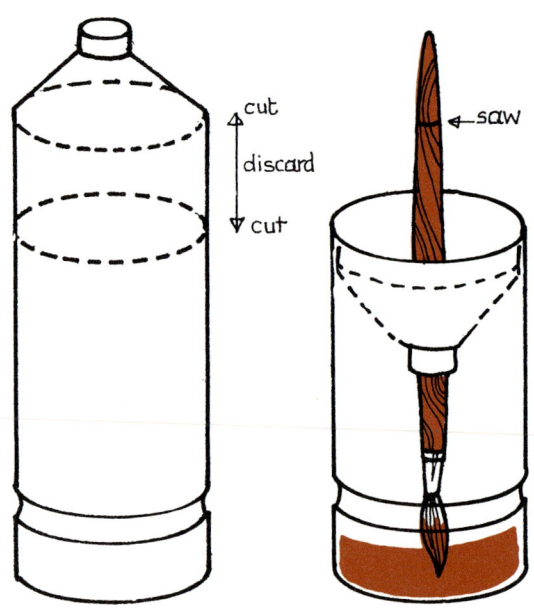

### A PAINT-POT TRAY

1  Take a seed box.
2  With a heated knife, cut two layers of polystyrene ceiling tiles to fit. Glue together. Test your glue first —some kinds melt polystyrene.
3  Place paint pots on tiles and draw around each base.
4  Cut out circles. Fit paint pots into holes.

### PAINT BRUSHES

A selection of shapes and sizes in artists' brushes. You may find it safer to cut down the long handles and sandpaper the ends smooth. Look after brushes: clean them regularly, smooth the hairs back into shape, and stand them in a container with brushes up, handles down.

### EASEL

The necessity for scrubbing down an accumulation of thick dried-on paint can be reduced by covering the board with kitchen foil.

Provide a selection of large crayons, felt-tip pens, pencils and ballpoints as well as paint and brushes for the children to experiment with. All have their uses.

### PAPER

Sugar paper, newsprint, end rolls of newspaper from the printers, tissue paper, gummed coloured squares, soft toilet paper for wiping spills and noses, paper towels for drying hands, books of out-of-date wallpaper samples.

A 60 cm (approximately 24") ruler is invaluable for cutting up large sheets of paper into suitable sizes for painting.

30 cm (approximately 12") ruler, tape measure.

## CARDBOARD

Use cereal packets.

Grocery cartons of thick cardboard can be used as large building bricks for making a wall. They can also be used for storing things.

Use the largest carton you can find for drip-drying paintings. Make holes and thread garden wire across top. Peg on paintings. The bottom of the box catches the drips. It can be folded flat for storage.

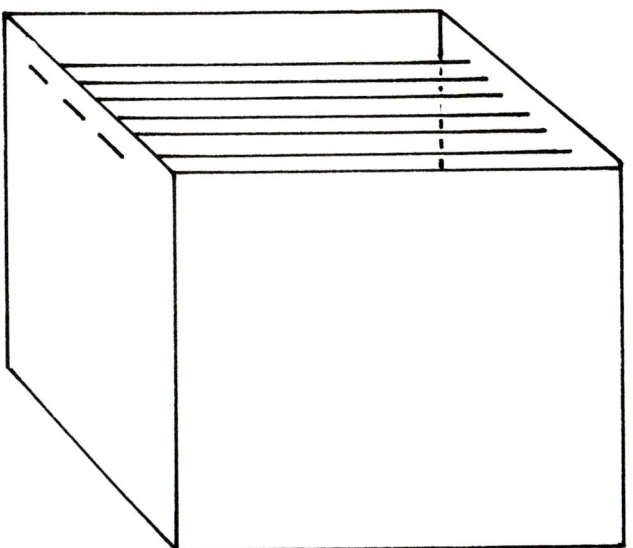

## GLUE

You will need a non-toxic, strong bonding glue that washes off clothing, like white school glue or an equivalent. UHU and Bostik are stronger. Copydex for felt work and cloth collages. When you buy balsa wood ask for the best glue to go with it. Wallpaper paste thickens paint and makes papier mâché. Use paste in a push-up stick form for quick sticking without mess. Gummed labels, sticky tape, special putty for displaying children's artwork on walls. Gummed brown paper strip, Passé partout and tough tape come in useful. Glue can be dispensed in liquid detergent paint pots with brushes.

## MISCELLANEOUS

Stapler
Hole punch
Garden wire
Pipe cleaners (extra long and furry coloured ones can be ordered from educational suppliers)
Clay
Kitchen foil
String
Pastry
Sand and water trays
Large beads for threading
PVC aprons
Phosphorescent road safety arm bands can be ordered from ROSPA
Royal Society for the Prevention of Accidents,
Royal Oak Centre,
Brighton Road,
Purley,
Surrey CR2 2UR

# JANUARY week 1

## TO TALK ABOUT

New year's day is the birthday of the year that has just begun. Have the children seen any new year greeting cards with a picture of a new baby on them? Maybe mothers could spare some Christmas and new year cards for sorting games at playgroup. Count with the children the number of pictures of the 'new year baby' they find in greeting cards, magazines and newspapers.

Do any of the children in your group have a birthday close to new year's day? Does anybody have a new baby sister or brother to talk about?

## TO LOOK FOR

### Red for the colour table

Red is the first colour in the rainbow. What can the children tell you about it?

Red is a warm, bright, cheerful, strong colour. It is the colour of Father Christmas's clothes. It is the colour of warming (and dangerous) fire. It is the colour of robin red breasts and holly berries. It can be the colour of noses in winter.

Red is often used as a warning of danger. It is the colour of a stop-light.

Red is a primary colour. You cannot create it by mixing two other colours together. If you mix red and white paint you make pink paint.

## TO JOIN IN

### Movement

January 6 is the twelfth night after Christmas. It is customary to take Christmas decorations down by the 6th, which is Epiphany, a Christian festival celebrating the visit of the three wise men bearing gifts for baby Jesus. Some of the children might find it fun to use the streamers and tinsel you are taking down to help them dress up like wise men. Christmas card nativity scenes will give them an idea of what they are supposed to look (and feel) like. How did people long ago walk in flowing robes without tripping? Let the children try walking a little way in long dressing-up clothes (not up and down stairs, please). They will soon discover that they have to take small, gliding steps, and keep one hand free for holding the skirt clear of their feet as they walk. Now that the children have thought about what they are doing, and found a method of coping, they should be less likely to trip accidentally. Add dignified music. A slow beat on a tambourine is sufficient.

The wise men followed a star in the sky which led them to Jesus.

### Rhymes

'Twinkle, twinkle, little star' (THE BOOK OF A THOUSAND POEMS).

Star light, star bright,
First star I see tonight,
I wish I may, I wish I might,
Have the wish I wish tonight.
(Make a wish.)

Oh, I am the Man in the Moon,
Won't you visit me soon?
Should you be taking a trip to the stars
Please drop in on the way to Mars,
Morning or afternoon.

Rose Fyleman

*The Night Sky*
All day long
The sun shines bright.
The moon and stars
Come out by night.
From twilight time
They line the skies
And watch the world
With quiet eyes.

Riddle: Higher than a house,
Higher than a tree,
Oh, whatever can that be?
Answer: A star.

**Songs**

'Wynken, Blynken and Nod' and 'Away in a Manger'
(words in THE BOOK OF A THOUSAND POEMS)

## TO INVESTIGATE

Do the children know what their 'birthday suit' is?
What other things that adults say puzzle them?

## TO CREATE

### Shape pictures

Sit with the children and see if they can work out
how to make a six-point star by placing one triangle
of paper across another. Look at Christmas wrapping
paper together. How many shapes can the children
find to cut out? They might find bells, stars, Christmas ball circles, Christmas tree triangles, Christmas
box squares and rectangles. Draw around these
shapes on coloured paper and cut out to make
abstract shapes. Each child can glue his collection
of shapes on plain paper to make a montage. Make
time to listen when the children want to talk about
their pictures. Print each child's name on his picture
with a capital first letter, the rest in small letters,
e.g. John. Print something he has told you about his
picture, if he wishes you to.

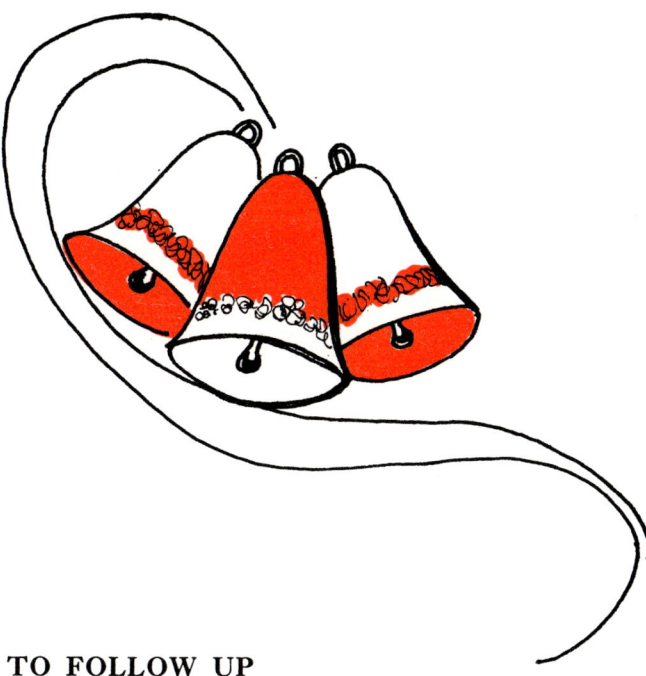

## TO FOLLOW UP

### Look for the moon

Have the children noticed that the moon can sometimes be seen in the daytime? Next time you go for
a walk, look for the pale daytime moon and note the
way it seems to follow you around, disappearing
behind rooftops and reappearing between houses, as
if it were playing hide and seek.

The stars are especially bright in winter, and they
appear earlier and closer to bedtime than in summer.
They feed a child's awakening sense of fantasy and
interest in science, and are particularly relevant to
this space-age generation.

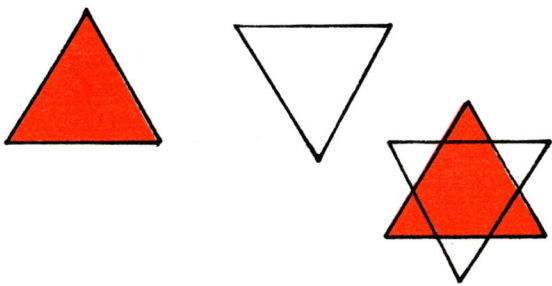

## TO TALK ABOUT

### Old Father Time

We think of the new year as a new baby. We think of the old year as an old man, a grandfather. This old man is sometimes called Old Father Time. In pictures he is usually shown carrying an hour-glass and a scythe. Can the children find any pictures of Old Father Time on new year's cards or in magazines? Greeting cards are a rich source of folk-lore symbols that are a kind of picture shorthand for an event, and, therefore, useful to understand. The picture of a stork delivering a baby often mystifies modern children.

## TO LOOK FOR

### Fruit in the shops now

The variety of fruit available in January is limited, but you can still see oranges, lemons and apples at the greengrocer's. The vitamin C in oranges is especially necessary to children in winter when they cannot absorb enough of it from the sun.

Try sculpting the rind of an orange into little ears and a pig's snout before you peel it. Make a hole in the top of an orange and push a sugar lump right inside. The lump will dissolve and the juice can be sucked ready-sweetened. A wedge of orange peel can be cut to make false teeth.

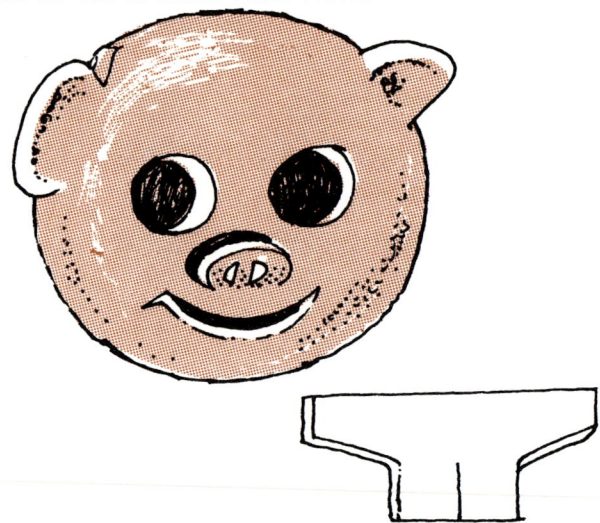

An old superstition says that if you peel all the skin off an apple in one long piece and throw it over your left shoulder, it will fall in the shape of the first letter of the name of your sweetheart. Little children could try to form the first letter in their own names out of apple peel. The peel is just as good for you as the apple itself. Advise children to wash each apple before eating.

## TO JOIN IN

### Movement

What would it feel like to be an old man like Father Time? What is a scythe and how is it used? These are movements the children could explore this week.

An old man might shuffle in his slippers. He might hunch up his shoulders against the cold. He might shiver to warm himself, and rub his hands together to help the circulation. His teeth might chatter on a very cold day. His head might nod.

A game to play: Oranges and Lemons (in THE OXFORD NURSERY SONG BOOK).

## Traditional stories

'Little Red Riding Hood' and 'The Three Pigs' both contain a time element and could be accompanied by the warning 'don't talk to strangers'. Make the most of the repeated phrases, encouraging the children to join in. Tell the least horrific version. A timid or easily frightened child might have a vivid imagination that makes the stories seem real.

## Songs

'The Bells of London' (THE PUFFIN BOOK OF NURSERY RHYMES)

'My Grandfather's Clock' (CHILDREN'S FAVOURITES, record MFP1175)

Count on fingers to 'One man went to mow' and 'This old man came rolling home' (THE OXFORD NURSERY SONG BOOK)

## Action rhymes

'Hickory, dickory dock' (PUFFIN BOOK OF NURSERY RHYMES)

Can you walk on tiptoe,
As softly as a cat?
Can you stamp along the road,
Stamp! Stamp! Just like that?
Can you take some great big strides,
Just like a giant can?
Or walk along so slowly
Like a poor old, bent old man? Can you?

'There was a crooked man' (PUFFIN BOOK OF NURSERY RHYMES)

## TO INVESTIGATE

## Clocks

Do the children know how an hour-glass works? Perhaps a mother could lend an egg-timer that works the same way for the children to watch. Time it with a kitchen timer, if one can be brought, to reinforce the idea of how long four minutes is.

How many children have seen a grandfather clock and heard it chime? How many have seen a grandmother clock, smaller and daintier? A cuckoo clock? A sundial? How many have been woken by an alarm clock ringing in the morning. Can an old broken clock be spared for taking apart? If so, provide a small screw-driver (this is a sitting-down activity) and a tray for collecting all the pieces. Check that springs are removed safely.

## TO CREATE

### A kitchen clock

Use a round biscuit tin to trace a circle on cardboard, or use paper plates. An adult can lightly pencil in the numbers 1 to 12. Each child can crayon over the numbers according to ability. An adult will need to make long and short cardboard hands and fasten them in the centre of the clocks with a paper fastener. Although most of the work is done for the child, he is learning about shape, space and numbers, and becoming familiar with the idea of a long and short hand and the direction in which they move.

### A grandfather clock

A clock face can be pinned up in the home corner, or pasted on a cardboard grocery carton to make a grandfather clock. A square box at the top and bottom, and a long, narrow box in the middle form the body of the clock. This provides a good opportunity for a painting and decorating job on the cartons. Use large pots of paint and wide, thick brushes. Powder paint mixed with undiluted liquid detergent will cover most printing on cartons. Remember to protect the floor with plastic sheeting or newspapers. It makes cleaning up much easier.

### Paste-on numbers

Large numbers cut from last year's calendar are useful for making clocks, for charts and number work.

## TO FOLLOW UP

### 'What's the time, Mr Wolf?'

In this game all the children creep up behind the one who is chosen to be Mr Wolf. They go a little way, stop and chant, 'What's the time, Mr Wolf?' Mr Wolf answers without turning around, '1 o'clock!' The children creep a little closer and chant again. Mr Wolf might answer, '3 o'clock!' When Mr Wolf thinks he can tell by the voices that a child is close enough for him to catch, he shouts, 'dinner time', turns and runs after the children, trying to catch one who will then become the next Mr Wolf. (For under-fives, it is best if an adult is Mr Wolf all the time.)

# JANUARY week 3

## TO TALK ABOUT

### Springs

Last week the children may have found tiny springs in an old clock. This week they could try to think of other things that have springs. For instance, the cord between receiver and telephone is springy. Some hair rollers have springs in them. Beds have springs. Retracting ballpoint pens have springs inside.

You could show the children how a spring can be made, by winding plastic-covered garden wire around a pencil and then slipping it off the end. Warn the children that, besides being useful, springs can be dangerous if not handled sensibly.

## TO LOOK FOR

### Plant life

Falling larch needles, falling oak leaves, winter jasmine, snowdrops, holly, ivy, mistletoe.

Look for red berries. Warn children that many berries are poisonous. They must *never* try to eat berries they have picked without adult supervision.

At this time of year we can see tree shapes clearly by their bare branches. The children could use fallen oak leaves and cottonwool snow to make a montage of this month. Provide plenty of snippets of interesting material so that imagination is not confined to a set subject. See if anyone can find a leaf skeleton.

## TO JOIN IN

### Movement

Send a group of the oldest children off to count how many doorways they can pass through in your hall or home.

Folk dance: 'In and out the windows' (WALLY WHYTON'S GOLDEN HOUR OF NURSERY RHYMES, Pye Records). If this is explained to the children, then practised step by step before being put together, it can be fun, although not everyone may want to join in. At least two adults are needed to help position children.

The children stand in two rows, facing each other in pairs. They can measure the right distance between each other by stretching arms and touching hands, in front, then to the sides.

Sing: Stand and face your partner,
      Stand and face your partner,
      Stand and face your partner,
      As we have done before!

Now the children form two rows of arches by raising their arms sideways. The first child in each row skips in and out of the arches.

Sing: In and out the windows,
      In and out the windows,
      In and out the windows,
      As we have done before.

The two partners stand and face each other again at the end of the row. All lower arms, take one pace upwards to keep the rows in the same place, and begin again. Continue until everybody has had a turn of going in and out of the windows, and the first couple are back at the first position in their rows, or until the children tire of it. Have a rest!

In another version, children join hands in a ring. One child begins going 'in and out the windows' of arched arms. He chooses a partner, then they change places. Choose the version that seems most suited to your children. In a large group not everybody might have a turn of going in and out the windows with the circle version.

How high can the children reach with their up-stretched arms? How could they reach even higher? By jumping! Try to jump! To get a really good, high jump you must first coil yourself down and then fling yourself up like a spring.

### Action rhyme

The children crouch for first two lines, then spring up on last line.

Jack in the box is a funny wee man—
He sits in his box as still as he can (pause)
Then UP he pops!

How many ways can the children think of to spring about? They could spring from one foot to the other. They could spring like a kangaroo. They could spring like a bullfrog. They could do a springy, slow-motion walk like astronauts walking on the moon with no gravity to hold them down. Perhaps somebody could lend an old foam rubber cot mattress for trampoline practice.

## TO INVESTIGATE

### A height chart

It is interesting to see how much small children grow in a year. Ask each in turn to stand up against a doorframe, and measure the height. Make a note of each child's height. Cut used Christmas wrapping paper into 10 cm (4") squares. Now give each child a long length of strong, one-ply toilet paper. Give each the appropriate number of squares to glue on his length of toilet paper. Rule any extra centimetres in when the glue has dried. There are sure to be gaps because the children will not be able to position the squares exactly. Just tuck in the gaps and staple them. The result will be a fairly approximate height chart. The children will gain some experience of the size of a 10 cm (4") square, and the usefulness of measurement. How tall are their dolls? How tall is the cat?

### Flour and water paste

Sift some flour and a little salt into a bowl. Make a well in the middle. Slowly pour on cold water, stirring to a creamy texture.

For stronger glue, add more water to make a thinner mixture, then boil for a few minutes to thicken, stirring constantly. You can add powder paint and use it for finger painting or for thick brush-on paint.

## TO CREATE

### Jumping Jacks

Tiny tots can make a Jack in a matchbox by concertina-folding a strip cut from a greeting card. Sticky-tape a funny face (cut from a greeting card or magazine, or drawn) on one end. Tape the other end inside a matchbox drawer. When you slide the matchbox open the Jack will jump out.

Another kind of Jumping Jack can be made from cereal packets. Cut off the flaps of some empty cereal packets. Fold the packets flat and cut in sections widthways. The children can glue the sections one on top of another. Glue the bottom section to the front of a whole cereal box for stability. Cut a saucer-size circle and paint a face on it. Glue on spikey-cut crêpe paper hair. Glue the face to the top section. When the glue has dried, the children can press Jack down flat and watch him spring up again, or they can hold the bottom packet and swing Jack in and out like a concertina.

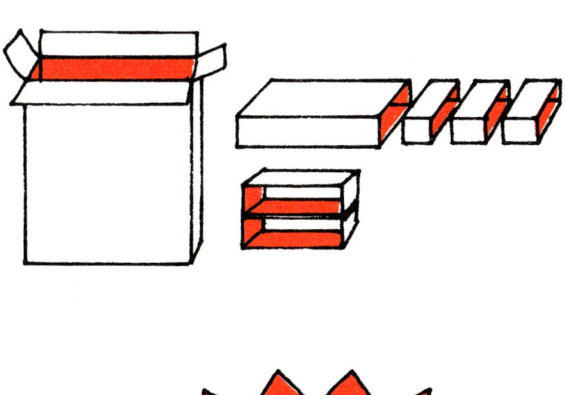

For another Jack-in-a-box and a paper-fold puppet, see 'Things for adults to make'.

## TO FOLLOW UP

Children could bring toys to show and talk about that demonstrate springiness. For example, balancing toys that contain a lead weight that makes them spring back upright when pushed over; weighted toys that tumble down a slope; a spring that 'walks' down stairs; real Mexican jumping beans; a Jack-in-a-box; spring scales; clockwork toys and music boxes.

# JANUARY    week 4

## TO TALK ABOUT

### Keeping warm

All this month small creatures will be hibernating, curled up asleep in cosy nests they have made, until the coldest weather is over.

Have the children noticed that pets, like rabbits and cats, grow extra thick coats in winter to keep them warm? How do the animals take off their thick coats when warm weather comes? You could explain that they moult. The extra hair thins out so they will be cool in summer. Sheep grow extra thick wool to keep them warm in winter. They are glad to have this thick wool sheared off for the summer and we are glad to have the wool to make into coats and jumpers to keep us warm in winter.

The children might find scraps of fleece in a field where sheep graze. Can they feel the grease in it? That is natural oil to stop rain from soaking the sheep. Wash the fleece with detergent to make it white and fluffy.

## TO LOOK FOR

### Wildlife

Watch for robins and the blue-tit. Put out food for the birds.

### Weather

January is the coldest month of the year. The temperature will be very low. Snow is likely to fall. Icicles may form along the edge of overhanging roofs.

There is a rhyme that helps to remind us of average centigrade temperatures:

Five and ten and twenty-one,
Winter, spring and summer sun.

A seasonal warning: winter is the peak time for burning accidents. Warn children never to go too near unguarded fires, or play with matches. Make sure they cannot do these things on your premises.

## TO JOIN IN

### Movement

Let the children pretend to be snowflakes swirled by the wind, now drifting gently, and finally settling comfortably on the floor.

### Nursery rhymes

'The north wind doth blow' (see March, week 1)
'Mary had a little lamb'
'Little Bo-peep'
'Baa, baa black sheep'
(All in THE PUFFIN BOOK OF NURSERY RHYMES)
'White sheep, white sheep, on a blue hill,' a riddle in rhyme (see March, week 1)

January brings the snow,
Makes our feet and fingers glow
                              Sara Coleridge

### Action rhyme

Two little dickie-birds sitting on a wall,
One named Peter, the other named Paul.
Fly away Peter, fly away Paul.
Come back Peter, come back Paul.

Draw a bird face on the nail of the index finger on both hands. When Peter and Paul fly away, raise hand and tuck finger under, substituting middle finger, then change when 'birds' come back. You could do this using thimbles, leading into a game of Hunt the Thimble where searchers become 'warmer' as they get closer to the hiding place and 'colder' as they move away. Hand plays are useful for amusing children on long car journeys. You will find more in February, week 3.

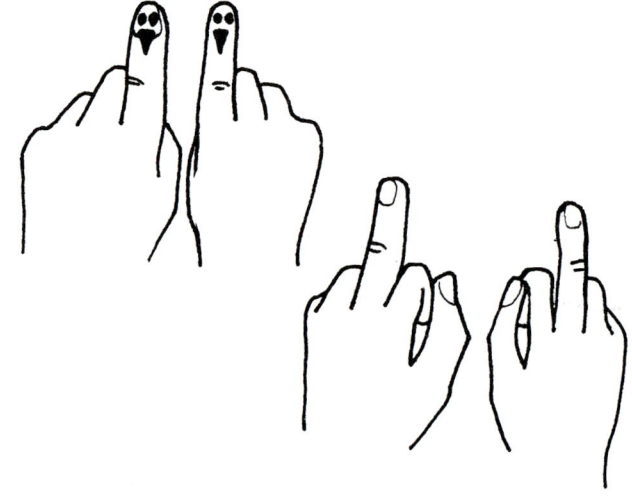

### Songs

'The Grand Old Duke of York' (THE BOOK OF A THOUSAND POEMS)

Oh, we can play on the triangle,
And this is the music to it,
Ting, ting, ting, ting, ting, ting, ting,
And that's the way we do it!

(Music in THIS LITTLE PUFFIN)

Lots of vigorous activity is needed to keep the children warm in January. Let them shake their fingers to feel them glow. Clap hands, stamp feet. Be soldiers marching down the street to marching tunes. Add the sounds of instruments, bought or home-made, if you have them.

### Story

'Dame Trot and her pig that wouldn't get over the stile.' One version, with pictures by Paul Galdone, is called THE OLD WOMAN AND HER PIG. Another version, called 'An Old Rhyme', is in THE BOOK OF A THOUSAND POEMS.

### TO INVESTIGATE

#### The temperature

Do you have an outdoor minimum-maximum thermometer? It is interesting to look at one of these with the children every month to see how the temperature changes through the year. You could show this fluctuation with a simple graph for the wall. This month the mercury is likely to be at its lowest.

Here are some puzzles to set the children thinking: How do we know it is cold, even if we don't have a thermometer? We can *feel* it is cold. How else can we find out about things if there is nobody around to tell us? We can taste, hear, see, and smell. If snow falls, encourage the children to taste the falling flakes with their tongues. Look through a magnifying glass at a snowflake that has alighted on a dark coat.

If we feel a cold wind blowing on us, how can we find out which direction it is blowing from? One way is to put a finger in your mouth to wet it all over, then hold it up. The side that dries first is the side that the wind is blowing from. Work out which direction that is with a pocket compass. Children are fascinated by the mechanical action of the arrow long before they understand how it works.

There may be a weather vane on top of a nearby building, with a weather cock being blown around to point north, south, east or west. In which direction are the clouds moving?

### TO CREATE

#### Potato animals

The children could make some lambs, robins, a farmer, and many make-believe animals using potatoes, matchsticks, large beads, plasticine, brass paper fasteners, buttons, cotton reels, cottonwool, pipe cleaners, feathers and coloured wood spills. If you have a large group of children to cope with, you need to be really organised. Prepare name-tags for the creations in advance, or write each child's name on a large sheet of paper and stand all that child's creations on it ready for going home.

### TO FOLLOW UP

Test centrifugal force by whirling a basket and its contents upside-down on a piece of string. If you do it fast, the contents won't fall out—they seem to stick to the bottom of the basket.

Test balance, the equal distribution of weight, on balance scales; on a see-saw.

Gain momentum on a swing.

Study inertia, the running down of stored energy, with a spinning top.

### Look at

USE YOUR SENSES series (Burke Books)
THE FIVE SENSES, by Aliki (A. & C. Black)

## TO TALK ABOUT

### Candlelight

In winter we sometimes have to switch on the light even in the daytime because the sky is dark. Everybody uses so much more electricity in the winter than in the summer that we sometimes have a power cut. There is not enough power to supply everybody at the same time. Have the children in your group experienced a power cut recently? Most children revel in the atmosphere and inconvenience of candlelight. Can the children imagine what it must have been like before electric light was invented, when people had only candles and oil lamps to light their homes at night?

## TO LOOK FOR

### Orange for the colour table

Orange is the second colour in the rainbow. Orange is a warm, cheerful, sunshine colour, often linked with yellow and gold. It is the colour of a flickering candle flame. It can be the colour of the setting winter sun. Orange can be made by mixing red and yellow. Many different shades can be produced by varying the amount of red or yellow, and by adding a little white or black. Amber is the colour of the 'caution' traffic light. Flowers often have orange stamens. Falling leaves can be orange. An orange is orange. How many different textures can the children find around them in the colour orange?

## TO JOIN IN

### Movement

Here is a riddle in rhyme. Can the children guess what it is?

Little Nanny Etticoat
In a white petticoat
And a red nose.
The longer she stands,
The shorter she grows.

The answer is a candle, melting slowly as the wick burns. Have the children noticed this happening to candles on a birthday cake? They might like to pretend to be birthday candles, standing tall and straight. No wobbling! Count how many children there are to find out how old the birthday person would be. Now go around and pat each child on the head to 'light' the candles. Slowly, slowly the 'candles' sink down to the floor as the wax melts. Solemn chords on the piano help this effect.

Here is another rhyme that can be a game.

Jack be nimble,
Jack be quick,
Jack, jump over the candlestick.

This can be played with a skipping rope held between two adults. Start with it very low for the tiny tots, then gradually raise it to see who can jump the highest, chanting the rhyme each time that somebody is about to jump.

Transform the rope into a snake or waves on the ocean by making 'wriggles' or 'waves' travel from one end to the other.

### Nursery rhymes

To make your candles last for aye,
You wives and maids give ear-O!
To put them out's the only way,
Says honest John Boldero.

How many miles to Babylon?
Three score miles and ten!
Can I get there by candlelight?
Yes, and back again!
If your heels are nimble and light,
You can get there by candlelight.

## TO INVESTIGATE

### Some uses for wax (for an adult to show to a child)

*Mosaics*

Save small crayon ends. They can be grated, minced or pencil-sharpened into small multi-coloured pieces suitable for gluing into mosaics.

*A doll's face*

To finish off a simple rag doll, draw a face with coloured wax crayons directly on cloth. Press with a hot iron. The image will become semi-permanent, lasting through several mild washings. Special fabric crayons give a brighter result.

*Transfers*

After the children have finished a session crayoning on paper, transfer their drawings onto an old sheet. Put the drawings face down on the sheet and press with a hot iron. Cut up and use for doll's bedspreads and tablecloths. Greaseproof paper makes a clearer transfer than absorbent paper.

## Finger-painting

Before you start a finger-painting session, rub all over the paper with a piece of candle. It prevents the paper from becoming soggy, and helps the fingers to glide smoothly.

## Finger-paint recipe

Mix flour, a little salt, and water to a creamy consistency. Add powder paint and blend to a good strong colour. (Starch or soapflakes are not suitable for children who are likely to put fingers in their mouths.)

## TO CREATE

### A rag doll

Most little children would love to make a real rag doll for themselves. This will require some preparation by you, but the child can still feel that she has made the doll herself. You can use the pattern on page 109, or make one of your own.

Draw a simple doll shape with crayon on wax-resistant paper. In a different colour draw a broken line cutting guide 1.5 cm (approx. $\frac{3}{4}$″) outside the body outline. Transfer by ironing onto cloth—an old piece of sheet is ideal. Draw over your doll outlines on paper again with crayon. Transfer this to another piece of cloth. Now you have an identical front and back. Crayon a doll's face on one head part. Place it face down on a piece of paper (to protect your ironing board cover) on your ironing board, and press with a hot iron. Print the child's name on the chest, directly on cloth. Press again.

Quite young children will be able to cut out such a doll with pinking shears, leaving a hem edge. Pin, staple or tack the front and back pieces together. Now the child can stitch roughly around the inner outline, leaving a space where scraps of cloth can be put in for loose stuffing. After stuffing the doll, the child can stitch up the opening and stitch across where arms and legs join the body, to give movement. For hair, lay lengths of yarn across a piece of clear sticky tape, then stick it on the doll's head. As young children's attention span is short, the doll could be made over several sessions.

## TO FOLLOW UP

### Wax-resist

Give the children pieces of candle to draw with. When they have had a good scribble, let them brush watery paint all over the page. The wax outline should show through because the wax resists being covered by water-based paint. Try again, using coloured wax crayons instead of a candle.

### Textures

Sticky-tape coins to a sheet of paper. By rubbing the paper side with crayon the children can reproduce their own 'coins' for playing shop. Now let them try rubbing a crayon on a piece of paper covering different textured surfaces, such as wood grain, open weave fabric, or small floor tiles. How many textures can they find to experiment with, indoors and out?

### Wax scratch pictures

Let each child cover a sheet of paper with solid colour using large chubby crayons. Next, cover the colour with black. They then scratch lines in the black. The other colour shows through to make a picture. For scratchers use Dad's plastic collar stiffeners or ordinary hair grips.

# FEBRUARY week 2

## TO TALK ABOUT

### R for rain

February has two country names, Fill Dyke and Sprout Kale; Fill Dyke because much rain and melting snow fill the waterholes, and Sprout Kale because cabbages begin sprouting. If you rule up a simple weather chart and draw an appropriate symbol each day, the children will be able to see clearly just how wet February can be. See sample chart on page 110.

There is a saying that we can expect plenty of rain if there is an 'R' in the name of the month. Fill up a weather chart for each month to see if this is true. Check the weather note in the fourth week of every month in this book to see if the weather has been what we expect for the time of year.

## TO LOOK FOR

### Fruit in the shops now

Apples, oranges, pears, rhubarb

## TO JOIN IN

### Action song

*Dashing Away with the Smoothing Iron* (on record HMA229, 50 MORE ALL TIME CHILDREN'S FAVOURITES, with Wally Whyton).

'Twas on a Monday morning, when I beheld my
  darling,
She looked so neat and charming, in every high
  degree.
She looked so neat and nimble-O, A-washing of her
  linen-O,
Dashing away with the smoothing iron, dashing away
  with the smoothing iron,
She stole my heart away.

'Twas on a Tuesday morning, when I beheld my
  darling,
She looked so neat and charming, in every high
  degree.
She looked so neat and nimble-O, A-hanging out her
  linen-O,
Dashing away with the smoothing iron, dashing away
  with the smoothing iron,
She stole my heart away.

Next verses:
'Twas on a Wednesday morning—A-starching of her
  linen-O.

'Twas on a Thursday morning—A-ironing of her
  linen-O.

'Twas on a Friday morning—A-folding of her linen-O.

'Twas on a Saturday morning—A-airing of her
  linen-O.

'Twas on a Sunday morning—A-wearing of her
  linen-O.

This is a long song, but children enjoy the repetition. Explain unfamiliar words. Keep it interesting and lively. You can have lots of fun with it.

Begin with singing and acting out the different activities. Establish the clear 1, 2 beat with hand-clapping. Everybody march around the room to the tune! Sing 'dashing away with the smoothing iron' loud. Sing 'she stole my heart away' soft. Sing the first part of each verse slowly. Sing the second part fast. Piano accompaniment isn't necessary. You can clap out the rhythm, talk to the children, and set their feet marching at the same time. If your children do not have music regularly, try a variety of songs to capture their interest. Start and end the session with a familiar tune.

(Read MY KIND OF PLAYGROUP MUSIC, by Margaret Shephard, a PPA Publication.)

## TO INVESTIGATE

### Nesting time

This is the time of year when birds begin to choose their mates and build nests. Even in city streets you can hear the cooing of mating pigeons.

How many children in your group know where there is a bird's nest? Of course, they must not touch the nest or any eggs, but it would not hurt to peep into a nest if it were low enough. Each type of bird builds a slightly different kind of nest, but basically pieces of straw and twigs are woven together and lined with soft feathers. The children might like to try making nests like the birds. Besides straw and twigs they could use mud or clay. Lining could be made of feathers, hazel catkins or flower petals. Pebbles could be used for birds' eggs.

## TO CREATE

### A Valentine card

Just as the birds coo to each other in February, people like to send a greeting to someone they love on St Valentine's day, February 14. The children can make Valentine cards for their parents.

Cut large heart shapes out of stiff paper or thin cardboard for them. Provide a pile of magazines, old greeting cards, or flower seed catalogues for the children to cut pictures from, to paste on their cards. Rose petal paper confetti looks very attractive pasted on. What other possibilities can you and the children think of? Help the children to print their names on their cards; capital first letter, the rest in small letters, e.g. John. One heart can be glued on a lace paper doily, or two can be stapled together down each side, and a handle attached at the top to make a purse.

### A bird beak

1  Take a piece of paper about 20 cm (8″) square.
2  Fold in half.
3  Fold the two outer corners on one side in to meet at the centre of a triangle. Seal the join with sticky tape.
4  Turn over and repeat with the other side.
5  The bottom triangle fits over a child's thumb, top triangle fits over fingers, to make a pecking beak. Hold it in place with tabs of sticky tape.

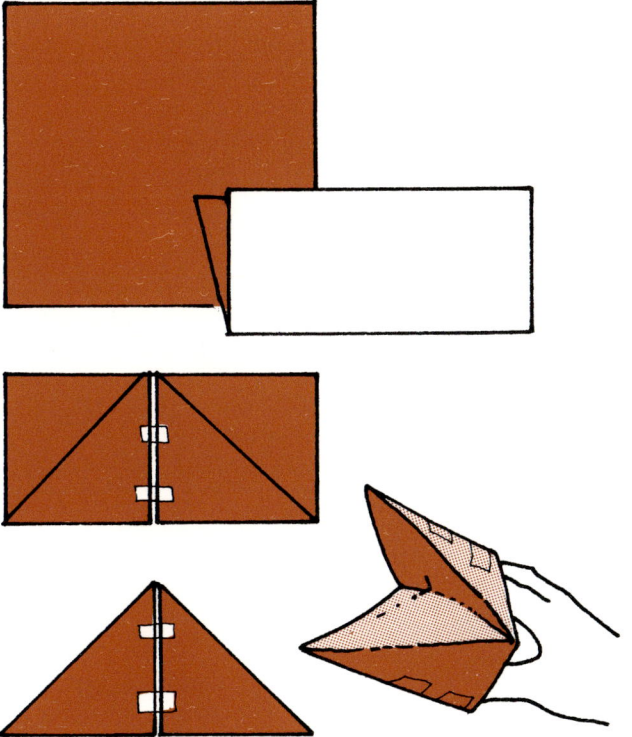

## TO FOLLOW UP

### Sing a guessing song

*The Green Grass Grew Around*

In a field there was a tree,
The finest tree you ever did see,
And the green grass grew around, around,
And the green grass grew around.

And on this tree there was a branch,
The finest branch you ever did see.
The branch was on the tree,
The tree was in the field,
And the green grass grew around, around,
And the green grass grew around.

And on this branch there was a nest . . .
And in that nest there were three eggs . . .
And on those eggs there sat a bird . . .

Sing to the children in a medium pitch, encouraging them to join in with the lines they know.

Have an easel near you. Sketch each new item on the easel as it is introduced in the song—the tree in the field with the green grass growing all around, then the branch, the nest, the eggs and the bird. You could also use a felt board.

After a few verses, stop singing after 'there was a' and wait for the children to tell you what each new thing is.

# FEBRUARY week 3

## TO TALK ABOUT

### Spring cleaning

In February all the countryside is washed clean by the soaking rain, ready for a fresh spring start. People, too, begin spring cleaning before the sunshine shows up the dust and grime of winter. The children can join in the bustle of cleaning activity, wiping down play tables and polishing chairs. Supply waterproof aprons. Give lots of scope for experimental water play.

## TO LOOK FOR

### Plant life

Crocus, snowdrop, cabbage sprouts, boxtree, daffodils. Fallen acorns start to sprout. The new shoot looks like a tiny creature emerging from an egg.

Daffy-down-dilly has come to town,
In a yellow petticoat and a green gown. (A daffodil)

## TO JOIN IN

### Action songs

This is the way we wash and scrub, wash and scrub, wash and scrub.
This is the way we wash and scrub on a cold and frosty morning.

(Children join hands and dance around in a circle for the chorus:)
Here we go round the mulberry bush, the mulberry bush, the mulberry bush.
Here we go round the mulberry bush, on a cold and frosty morning.

Make up other verses. (See THE OXFORD NURSERY SONG BOOK.)

Knees up, Mother Brown.
Knees up, Mother Brown.
Knees up, knees up,
Don't get the breeze up,
Knees up, Mother Brown.

### Rhymes

Tiny hands that have been playing with water should be dried and warmed before the children go out into the cold wind. Some hand-clapping rhymes will stimulate the circulation. See if the older children can manage to clap their own two hands together, then clap the right with the partner's right; own hands together, left with the partner's left, and so on. For younger children, clapping their own two hands together, then their partner's two hands, is difficult enough.

Pat-a-cake, pat-a-cake, baker's man.
Bake me a cake as fast as you can.
Pat it and prick it and mark it with T
And put it in the oven for Tommy and me.

Substitute the initial and name of one of the children in the group. Give each child a turn if they are enjoying it. Try to personalise rhymes wherever possible.

Try a hands, knees and boomps-a-daisy with partners.

1 busy housewife sweeping the floor
2 busy housewives polishing the door
3 busy housewives washing baby's socks
4 busy housewives winding up the clocks
5 busy housewives scrubbing out the sink
6 busy housewives giving puss a drink
7 busy housewives tidying the room
8 busy housewives shaking out the broom
9 busy housewives stirring the stew
10 busy housewives with nothing left to do.

Hold up a finger for each housewife, and do the appropriate action. Alternatively, each child could be a busy housewife, starting off his action as you pat him on the head. Do the action with him.

## TO INVESTIGATE

### Concentration

Ask the children to pat their heads and rub their tummies at the same time. It's hard to do. They will have to concentrate. Now do this: clasp your hands together tightly with fingers interlocked. Ask a child to point to whichever finger he would like you to raise, without touching that finger. You will be able to do it easily because you have had years of finger-brain coordination practice. The child won't find it quite so easy to lift the right finger the first time when it is his turn to try.

Now try this and see if the children can copy. Put the palms of your hands flat together. Bend the two middle fingers through between fingers of opposite hand. Slide your hands around so that middle fingers are at right angles to your arms. Wriggle the middle fingers in unison.

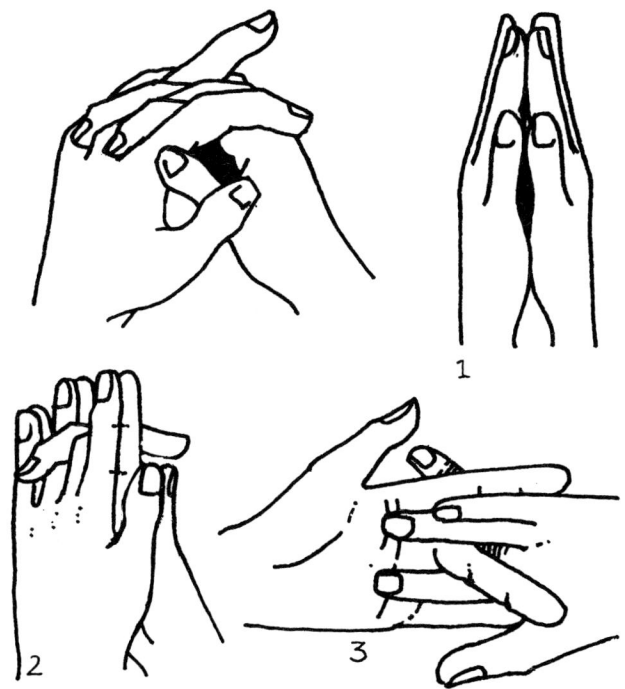

Can you do the Charleston, pretending to cross over your hands and knees? See if the children can work out how this is done!

## TO CREATE

### Swirly patterns

Perhaps the children have noticed patches of motor oil on wet asphalt, making rainbow-coloured patterns. Here's how they can make some swirly patterns. Cover the bottom of a shallow baking tray with water. The children can sprinkle on different coloured dry powder paints from a spoon. Swirl the water gently with a spoon. Now the children can 'take a print' off the surface of the water, by lightly placing a sheet of paper on top for a few seconds. This gives a pleasing marbled effect.

Submerge a piece of paper in the water. Remove it and sprinkle dry paint on the wet surface and spread it with the fingers.

For this next method you will need a small, well-controlled group if the children are not to end up looking like a tie-and-dye experiment gone wrong.

Mix a few drops of *waterproof* Indian Ink in water.

Place a sheet of blotting paper on the surface and let it soak up the water. Repeat with different coloured pieces of blotting paper and more and less Indian Ink.

Make blot pictures with water-based felt-tip pens on absorbent kitchen paper towels.

Hang up the patterns to dry (a supply of pegs in playgroup is invaluable), or spread them on layers of newspaper.

## TO FOLLOW UP

### Hand games

Tickly, tickly, on the hand,
If you laugh, you'll be a man.
If you smile, you'll be a lady.
If you cry, you'll be a baby.

Round and round the garden,
Like a teddy bear. (trace a circle on child's hand with index finger)
One step, two steps, (fingers walk up arm)
Tickly under there. (tickle under arm)

Here's the church. (clasp hands)
Here's the steeple. (raise two index fingers to meet)
Open the doors, (turn hands inside out)
And here's the people. (wiggle interlaced fingers)

Here's the lady's knives and forks. (fingers interwoven, backs of hands together)
Here's the lady's table. (fingers hidden, hands flat)
Here's the lady's looking-glass. (index fingers raised to meet)
Here's the baby's cradle. (raise little fingers to meet also)

### Toes game

This little pig went to market. (gently pull big toe)
This little pig stayed home. (gently pull 2nd toe)
This little pig had roast beef. (gently pull 3rd toe)
This little pig had none. (gently pull 4th toe)
And this little pig went wee, wee, wee, (gently pull little toe)

All the way home.

### Face game

Here sits the Lord Mayor! (touch forehead)
Here sit his two men! (touch eyelids)
Here sits the cock! (right cheek)
Here sits the hen! (left cheek)
Here sit the little chickens! (tip of nose)
Here they run in! (mouth)
Chinchopper, chinchopper, chinchopper, chin! (chuck the chin)

# FEBRUARY week 4

## TO TALK ABOUT

### Pancake day

Shrove Tuesday is traditionally 'pancake day'. It usually falls towards the end of February or beginning of March, depending on the dates for Easter. Pancakes provide an opportunity to eat up all the eggs in the larder before the fast of Lent. Most children love pancakes any time of year.

## TO LOOK FOR

### Weather

Lots of rain. Look at the outdoor thermometer. Does the mercury show that the temperature is a little higher than last month?

### Wildlife

Birds begin to nest. Squirrels end their hibernation and seek food.

## TO JOIN IN

### Movement

Expert pancake makers toss pancakes to turn them in the pan so that both sides are cooked. Ask the children to pretend to be holding a frying pan. Swing it up as if tossing a pancake high in the air. If it were a real pancake, they would follow it with their eyes, watching it go up and come down. Try to catch it in the frying pan! If the children gave the frying pan a big swing, the pancake might come down on the other side of the room. All run around, trying to 'catch' the pancake. Bang on a tambourine, or give a whistle, for when the pancake goes up . . . and when it comes down!

### Action rhyme

Mix a pancake, stir a pancake,
Pop it in the pan.
Fry a pancake, toss a pancake,
Catch it if you can.
Christina Rossetti

### Nursery rhymes

Hickety, pickety, my black hen,
She lays eggs for gentlemen.

Sometimes nine and sometimes ten,
Hickety, pickety, my black hen.

1, 2, 3,
Mother caught a flea,
Put it in a match-box
And made a cup of tea.
Flea jumped out,
Mother gave a shout,
In came Dad with his shirt hanging out.

## TO INVESTIGATE

### Kitchen science

The children may be used to playing with dry and wet sand. Have they felt the difference between dry and wet flour? Dry flour is fun to sift. It goes sticky when it is wet. Add more flour, and the children will be able to model with it, like plasticine. Salt improves the texture, and helps to preserve it. Add vegetable dye to make it more interesting.

Weigh a cupful of dry sand and a cupful of dry flour on balance scales to see how much lighter flour is. Try it with wet sand and wet flour. Both weigh more when water is added. The children could pour a measured amount of dry sand into different shaped containers—shallow, tall, round, square—and back into the measure to confirm that the shape changed but the amount remained the same.

Experiment with texture changes. Butter comes in a lump but can be beaten to a creamed consistency. The texture improves if sugar is added. Cream is runny, but it can be whipped into a solid form, and eaten with strawberry jam on pancakes.

### Play dough recipe

Mix two cups of salt with three cups of flour. Add a little water. Dust your hands with flour and knead the dough until it is pliable without being sticky.

## TO CREATE

### Pancakes

Ingredients:

100 g (4 oz) plain flour
250 ml (10 oz) milk
1 egg
pinch salt

Method:

1  Sieve flour and salt into mixing bowl. Make a well in the centre.

2  Add unbeaten egg and milk. Gradually draw in the flour, until a smooth batter is formed.

3  Beat well and set aside for half an hour if you can. Beat again lightly before using.

Pour out half a teacupful for each child. Each child can continue to beat his own pancake with a blunt fork. Children should take their mixture one at a time to the cooking area to have it cooked by an adult.

4  Melt a small piece of lard in a frying pan. When quite hot, and the pan is greased all over, pour in half a teacupful of batter.

5  Cook until the underneath is slightly brown. Turn and cook on the other side.

A pile of paper plates with names printed on, and a large shaker of sugar for children to sprinkle on the pancakes, will complete the feast.

## TO FOLLOW UP

### Collect kitchen implements

Set aside a 'kitchen' table for a week. Some of the things mothers might be able to loan are: scales, sifter, sieve, shaker, grater, grinder, peppermill, nutmeg grater, tea infuser, soap saver, rolling pin, tea strainer, colander, beaded milk-jug cover, funnel, timer, tin-opener, egg whisk, rotary egg beater, egg-slicer, potato masher, mincer, measuring spoons and jugs, wooden spoons, mortar and pestle, nut cracker, knife sharpener (whet stone), toast rack, condiment carrier, bowl scraper, soup ladle, sugar tongs, lemon squeezer, salad servers, teapot, coffee percolator, bottle brush, cork screw.

Items should have the owner's name or initials printed on a piece of paper and covered with sticky tape, to help the sorting out afterwards. They should also be old or indestructible. Introduce the children to the many fascinating pieces of kitchen equipment. Help them to understand the rules for using them, particularly safety rules. Tell them which things are dangerous, to be handled by adults only. Those things should be kept well out of reach, unless their use is being supervised.

### A boxing match

If you have children in the group who are forever fighting, fit them with oven gloves and let them work out their aggressions in a proper boxing match.

### Look at

PANCAKES, PANCAKES! by Eric Carle (Hamish Hamilton)

# MARCH week 1

## TO TALK ABOUT

### Stormy weather

March can be a stormy month, bringing the last snap of cold weather before spring really begins.

Have the children noticed that there are four main types of cloud we see in the sky? The dark nimbus clouds are the ones that bring heavy rain. It is interesting to watch the clouds change shape as they are blown by the wind. Sometimes they look like faces or animals. The children might like to make a painting of some clouds they have seen. Can they recall seeing clouds with the sun shining through in shafts, or clouds that cover the sun but have a silver or gold edge of sunshine?

When you are out for a walk, look for a lightning conductor on top of a church steeple. Mention that it is not a good idea to shelter under a tree in a thunderstorm.

## TO LOOK FOR

### Yellow for the colour table

Yellow is the third colour in the rainbow. It is the colour of sunshine and daffodils. If blue is added to yellow, the result is green. The children could try painting with yellow and blue only, making green where the colours overlap.

There are many different shades of yellow. It can be a vivid colour or a pale colour. The children could experiment with the whole range of yellows in tissue paper, tearing the tissue into pieces and pasting it on sugar paper to make sunshiny pictures. They could try scrunching the tissue up before gluing it on, for a three-dimensional effect. Stick a mass of yellow pictures on one wall and they will make the bleakest day seem bright. (You can obtain special putty from stationers that sticks pictures in place, and comes away without a mark when you want to take the pictures down.)

## TO JOIN IN

### Action rhyme

My little house won't stand up straight. (place
         fingertips of both hands together to make roof
                                 lean sideways)
My little house has lost its gate. (drop little fingers)
My little house rocks up and down. (rock 'house'
                                 from side to side)
My house is the oldest house in town.
And the wind blows ooooh . . . (blow through hands)
And the wind blows again ooooh . . . (blow through
                                 hands)
My house falls down. (drop hands in lap)
What a shame—what a shame! (wag head from
                                 side to side)

### Nursery rhyme

The north wind doth blow
And we shall have snow
And what will the robin do then, poor thing?
He'll sit in the barn
To keep himself warm
And hide his head under his wing, poor thing!
                         (cover head with arm)

### Nursery song

There was an old man called Michael Finnigan,
He grew whiskers on his chin-igan.
Along came the wind and blew them in again
Poor old Michael Finnigan, begin again . . .

### Poems

*Clouds*

I saw a lady in the sky today;
Her fleecy, floating skirts were long and wide,
Her arms were crossed, her head was turned away,
She had a dragon at her side.

A big grey dragon pawing in the air,
His curly tail went sweeping to the ground,
His mouth was open and his teeth were bare,
But he made no sound.

I turned to watch a butterfly go by,
And when I looked again where they had been—
The lady and the dragon in the sky—
They were not to be seen.
                                 Rose Fyleman

*White Sheep*

White sheep, white sheep
On a blue hill,
When the wind stops

You all stand still.
You all run away
When the winds blow;
White sheep, white sheep,
Where do you go?

## TO INVESTIGATE

### Weather lore

March is a windy month. Sara Coleridge wrote:

> March brings breezes loud and shrill,
> Stirs the dancing daffodil.

and the country saying is:

> As the days grow longer
> The winds grow stronger.

Have the children noticed that the days are getting longer and the nights are getting shorter as spring approaches?

There are other old sayings about weather, based on observation, that are usually correct:

A halo round the moon means strong winds.
A halo round the sun means rain.

Red sky at night, shepherd's delight.
Red sky in the morning, shepherd's warning.

Rain before seven, fine by eleven.

Clear moon, frost soon.

Mackerel sky and mares' tails
make tall ships carry low sails.
(Clouds that are broken up like fish scales and wispy tails may mean wind and rain on the way.)

You could try to 'whistle up' or 'whistle down' the wind. It's good practice for children just learning to whistle.

## TO CREATE

### Different kinds of whiskers

*Wood shavings*

May be obtainable from a local carpenter, or made with a piece of pine and a plane. The children will see all sorts of exciting possibilities in a pile of wood curls. They could sticky-tape them together to make beards and wigs, or simply feel them, and break them into tiny pieces.

*Paper curls*

Wind strips of paper taut around a pencil, then pull off to make them curl.

*Straw packing*

(Shredded wood or paper) Makes good whiskers to glue to a picture, or hair for a papier mâché puppet.

*Theatrical hair*

Some carnival novelty shops sell thin twirls of hair that can be teased out into beards, moustaches, and hair for puppets.

### Michael Finnigan

Ask a child to lie on a large sheet of paper on the floor. Draw around his outline. Now the children can stick a blowable beard on the drawing. Divide up paper-pulp egg cartons and let each child paint several cups. Glue the cups around and inside the drawn outline, so that each child has contributed something to making Michael Finnigan. Reserve three cups for eyes and nose.

## TO FOLLOW UP

### Newspaper whiskers

Show the children how to do this, and they may be able to do it by themselves.
1  Take a double newspaper page.
2  Leaving a 3 cm (1¼") strip at the centre fold, cut away ⅓ from either side of the page.
3  Cut the remaining ⅓ into narrow, frond-like strips, leaving the 3 cm (1¼") strip uncut at the top.
4  Place it around the chin and tie the strip at the back for King Neptune-type whiskers. (Good for mermaid grass skirts too.)

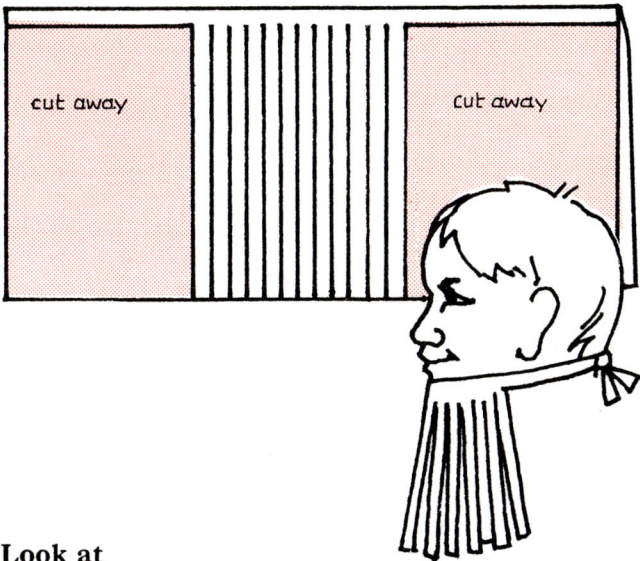

cut away          cut away

### Look at

HIGH IN THE SKY, by Althea (Dinosaur Books)
LITTLE BLUE AND LITTLE YELLOW, by Leo Léonni (Brockhampton)
CLOUDS, by Peggy Blakeley (A. & C. Black)

# MARCH week 2

## TO TALK ABOUT

### The life cycle of a tadpole

1 This month you may see small, jelly-like masses of frogs' eggs floating on the surface of ponds.

2 About a fortnight after the mother frog has laid her eggs, the tiny tadpoles hatch. They leave the jelly and attach themselves by suckers to pond weeds.

3 Next, three pairs of frond-like external gills develop and the mouth appears. The tadpole now feeds on a plant diet. The external gills disappear as gill slits develop.

4 After about a month the tadpole begins to grow hind legs.

5 The outer skin is shed, revealing front legs and eyes.

6 The tail is a storehouse of food. It becomes a stump and finally disappears altogether.

7 The fully-developed frog answers the call of the land. It can now live on insects it catches with a quick flick of its long tongue. Its tongue is actually a flap covered with sticky fluid, hinged to the lower jaw. The frog is an amphibian. That is the name given to creatures that can live on land or in water.

8 Next winter the frog will return to the pond and burrow deep into the mud. It will sleep there until the following spring. Then we will again hear its strange croaks, which are produced by air sacs near the throat. Perhaps the frog is calling 'more rain! more rain!' Frogs like wet weather. Too much sun might dry up their waterhole and shrivel their skin.

## TO LOOK FOR

### Fruit in the shops now

Apples, pears, rhubarb; imported peaches, oranges and bananas.

## TO JOIN IN

### Movement

Let the children pretend to be frogs and leap from their haunches. Croak (small hop), croak (small hop), croak (small hop), CROAK! (leap in the air after an imaginary fly).

Old saying: 'As scarce as frog's feathers.' Can the children guess why frog's feathers are scarce?

### Nursery songs

'A Frog went a-courting and he did ride, A-hum!' (CHILDREN'S FAVOURITES record MFP1175)

'A Frog he would a-wooing go. Heigh-ho, says Rowley.' (OXFORD NURSERY SONG BOOK, PUFFIN SONG BOOK)

'There's a frog on a log in a hole at the bottom of the sea.' (on record GROWING UP WITH WALLY WHYTON HMA245)

'The Little White Duck' (DANNY KAYE FOR CHILDREN, Coral Records)

### Story

'The Frog Prince', by Grimm

## TO INVESTIGATE

### Pond snails

Pond snails are generally more plentiful than tadpoles. They are interesting, and easy to keep. Like tadpoles, pond snails start life as a floating jelly-like substance. When they hatch they are very small and you must be careful not to empty them out with the change of water in your bowl. However, they soon grow if fed on goldfish food. They occasionally wander and you might find one some distance from the bowl, if it is a shallow one. When they are fully grown you may find fresh transparent 'jellies' on the side of the bowl, and the whole cycle begins again.

## TO CREATE

### A windmill

Demonstrate this step by step as the children copy, assisting them when necessary.

1 Take a 15 cm (6″) square of paper. Rule diagonal lines across from corner to corner. Make a cut 8 cm (3″) in from each corner towards the centre.

2 Take a long pin. Thread on a sequin or bead 'washer'. This will help the windmill to spin freely and prevent it coming off the pin head.

3 Bend the alternate side of each diagonal cut into the centre, slightly overlapping the corners.

4 Transfix all four corners and back of windmill with pin. Thread on a small cork, piece of drinking straw or bead 'spacer'. Secure the pin firmly to a smooth stick. Hold the windmill sideways into the wind to make it spin.

*Fishing net*
*Frog kite*  } See 'Things for adults to make'
*Bean bag*

## TO FOLLOW UP

### Keeping tadpoles

Children will need an adult to help them fish for frog spawn or tadpoles. They should not take too much.

Before your tadpole develops to stage 6, place a partly submerged rock or a twig log in the tadpole tank for him to bask on when he turns into a frog. Provide a few insects for his changed diet before his tail quite disappears. Return him carefully to the pond at a time when he won't be snapped up by hungry birds.

It is easy to believe Grimm's fairy story of the Frog Prince as you watch this handsome creature undergo so many fascinating transformations. Tadpoles will eat goldfish food and small pieces of raw mince. Do not overfeed. Introduce raw meat on a piece of string and remove it after an hour, so that it doesn't make the water sour. Change the water once a week, to keep the tank clean. Tap water should be left to stand for 24 hours before being used, to reach room temperature and to allow the chlorine to disperse. (This applies to goldfish too.)

### Log hopping

Lay out a row of sticks one in front of the other across the room.

Let the children try to walk from one end to the other without stepping on a stick. As they become more skilled they can try running, hopping, jumping, moving the sticks wider apart and closer together to make the game more difficult.

## TO TALK ABOUT

### Moss gardens

The soil usually remains damp throughout March. With the children, search for moss, which can be found growing in sheltered places.

Cut out matchbox size rectangles of moss, soil included. Transfer to a matchbox tray, and moisten. The children could add shamrocks they have found for St Patrick's Day.

Violets and daisies are beginning to appear now, along with bees to spread the pollen. The children could make buttonhole bouquets or moss gardens as gifts for Mother's Day.

If there is no moss, make 'imagination' gardens in kipper and herring tins (with no sharp edges), or plastic supermarket trays. Line with soil or wet sand. Collect twigs with a few leaves on for trees and logs, pieces of silver foil for ponds, grass for reeds.

Explain to the children that it is important not to pull up wild flowers by the roots, because some of them are becoming very rare.

## TO LOOK FOR

### Plant life

Primroses, celandines, periwinkles, narcissus, wood anemone, forsythia, iris. Budding now: pussy willow, ash, beech, larch, aspen, horse chestnut.

## TO JOIN IN

### Movement

March brings us the first day of official spring. The fresh fragrance in the air makes hares seem to 'go mad', romping and cavorting in the fields.

The children can pretend to be happy March hares. Place hands on the floor, kick legs to the sky. Jump up, run, spring onto hands and kick again.

Help the children to try doing hand-stands. Practise somersaults: let each child find a large space on a soft mat; rest on hands and knees, head tucked well under; now roll over forwards. All have a rest on the floor.

### Mother's Day poem

Roses are red
Violets are blue
Honey is sweet
And so are you.

### Action song

*Oats and beans and barley grow*

Chorus:
Oats and beans and barley grow,
Oats and beans and barley grow.
Not you, nor I, nor anyone knows,
How oats and beans and barley grow.

First the farmer sows his seed,
Then he stands and takes his ease,
Stamps his foot and clasps his hands,
And turns around to view the land.

(Repeat chorus)

(Music in THIS LITTLE PUFFIN)

### Poem

*In my garden*

In my little garden
By the apple tree,
Daffodils are dancing—
One—two—three!

In my little garden
By the kitchen door,
Daisies red are smiling—
Two—three—four!

In my little garden
By the winding drive,
Roses bright are climbing—
Three—four—five!

In my little garden
By the pile of bricks,

Hollyhocks are growing—
Four—five—six!

In my little garden
Down in sunny Devon,
Violets are hiding—
Five—six—seven!

In my little garden
By the cottage gate,
Pansies gay are shining—
Six—seven—eight!

Daffodils in golden gowns,
Daisies all in red,
Hollyhocks so very tall
By the garden shed,
Roses in the sunshine,
Violets dewy bright,
Pansies smiling gaily—
What a lovely sight!

### Story

'The Hare and the Tortoise', from AESOP'S FABLES

## TO INVESTIGATE

### Sowing time

You can buy packets of parsley, thyme and borage seeds for the children to plant now, if you would like to make a herb garden. Sage and chives grow from cuttings.

Plant nasturtium seeds now for hardy, bright flowers in summer.

This is the time to sow oats, barley, peas and beans.

If you are planting in a yogurt pot, make a hole in the bottom for drainage, and place it on a saucer. Place small stones in first, then cover with garden soil sieved by the children, or with John Innes potting compost. Water the soil before and after putting in the seed.

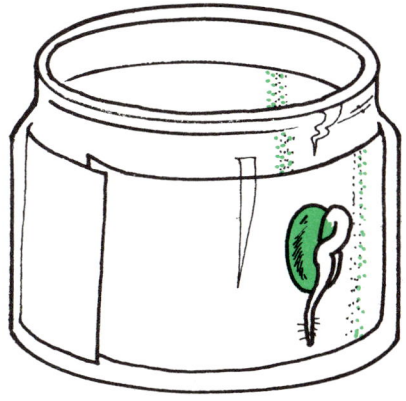

## Grow a bean on blotting paper

1 Soak a broad bean for a few hours until it becomes swollen.
2 Line a jar with a roll of blotting paper.
3 Place a broad bean between the paper and the jar, about half-way down.
4 Pour 2.5 cm (1″) of water into the jar. The blotting paper will soak this up. Always keep the blotting paper moist.
5 Germinate in a dark place, then bring into the light.

## TO CREATE

### An easy Mother's Day gift

Let the children cut corners off used envelopes. They can paint the corners or paste on pretty pictures from cards, magazines or flower catalogues. These make excellent bookmarks, fitted to the corner of a page.

### Cactus garden for nature table

Cactus plants begin to grow again in March. Their many shapes and textures appeal greatly to children. They can be laid out as a miniature garden in a large shallow bowl. The children can put in a mirror pond. Little china people or animals can be collected and moved about the garden by a child acting out some inner drama. Keep the garden in a light, sunny place.

## TO FOLLOW UP

### Growing miniature trees

This month apples and oranges are plentiful. Ask the children to save pips to plant. Push three orange pips about 1.3 cm (½″) into the soil in a yogurt pot. Keep in a light, warm room. Water often. As the seedlings grow, the children can replant them in larger pots. They won't grow fruit, but they look very pretty.

Apple seeds are not ready to be planted straight away. Put the pips in a jar with damp moss and keep them in a refrigerator for about six weeks. Turn them over occasionally until they start to sprout. Then treat as orange pips.

### Look at

GROWING THINGS, by Elizabeth Gundrey (Piccolo)

## TO TALK ABOUT

### A mystery box

Print 'mystery box' in lower case letters on a cardboard carton. Make a hole in it, large enough for a child's hand to fit in. Cover the hole with a glued-on curtain. Hang anything topical inside on a piece of string. See if the children can tell what the object is by feeling it. Ask them to describe what they can discover about the object, for example, 'it squeaks; it's soft; it has legs; it has whiskers'. Suggest other descriptive words that the children can test against the object, to stimulate language development. When everybody has had a guess, reveal what the object is and see who was right.

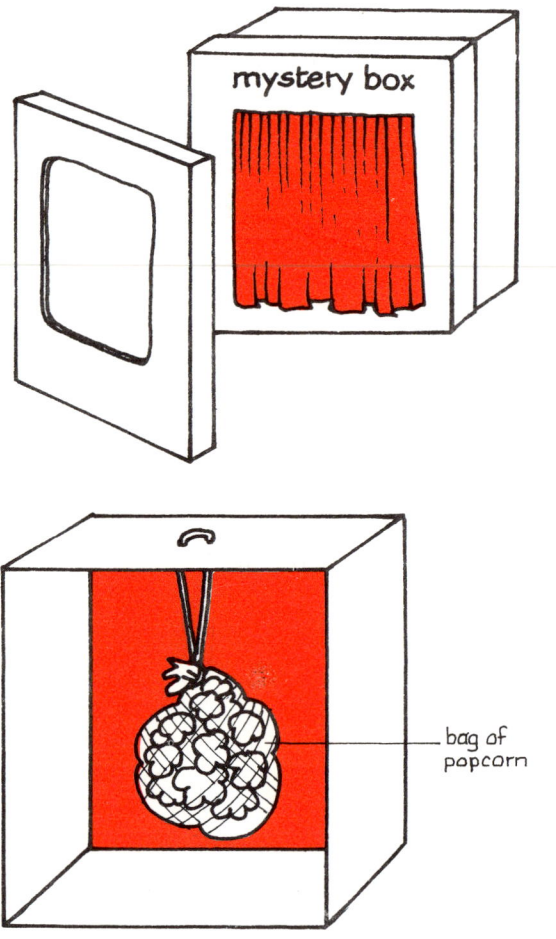

bag of popcorn

## TO LOOK FOR

### Wildlife

Song thrushes, blackbirds and hedge sparrows begin nesting. Hedgehogs and pet tortoises wake from hibernation. Squirrels build nests for the first litter of the year. Badgers clean their setts, ready for a new family. Look for frog spawn and pond snails in water holes. Look for lambs, calves and foals in the country. March hares romp in the fields.

### Signs that the weather is getting warmer

Check this month's temperature on the outdoor thermometer. Has it risen since you checked it at the end of last month, so that it now stands at about 10°C? Has March lived up to expectations, with high winds, storms, and some spring-like days? Did March 'roar in like a lion and go out like a lamb'?

## TO JOIN IN

### Movement

March 25 is the anniversary of the Angel Gabriel's visit to the Virgin Mary, telling her that she would be the mother of Jesus. The school playground game, 'Follow my Gable Oary Man', or 'Bangalory Man', is thought to have begun as 'I'll do everything I can to follow my Gabriel Holy Man', as little children of long ago strove to understand the adult church celebration through play-acting.

Pre-school children enjoy the simpler game of 'follow the leader'. They learn through trying out what it would feel like to be tall men, short men, rabbits, bears, kangaroos, fairies, giants, monkeys, etc., as the leader calls out the changes. Give the children the opportunity to think of some things themselves, and to be leaders. Music is not strictly necessary. The record of 'Zorba's Dance' is popular with children for background rhythm. Piano chords or tambourine are good for interpreting the difference in the types of movement.

'Here we go Lubin Loo' (music in THE PUFFIN SONG BOOK) and 'In and Out the Windows' (see January, week 2) have good skipping rhythms that can be adapted to heavy, light, fast and slow.

Records: 'Zorba's Dance', by M. Theodorakis, 'Carnival of the Animals', by C. Saint-Saëns.

## Nursery rhymes

'Tom, Tom, the Piper's Son'
'I Love Little Pussy'
'Ding, Dong, Bell!'
(All in THE PUFFIN BOOK OF NURSERY RHYMES)
'The Owl and the Pussy Cat', by Edward Lear
(THE BOOK OF A THOUSAND POEMS)

*The Kilkenny Cats*

There once were two cats of Kilkenny.
Each thought there was one cat too many;
So they fought and they fit,
And they scratched and they bit,
Till, excepting their nails,
And the tips of their tails,
Instead of two cats, there weren't any.

## Song

'Bought me a Cat' (Cat went fiddle-I-fee), from AMERICAN FOLKSONGS FOR CHILDREN, by Ruth Crawford Seeger

## Stories to read

'WHERE THE WILD THINGS ARE', by Maurice Sendak
'THE KING, THE MICE AND THE CHEESE', by Nancy and Eric Gurney
'MILLIONS OF CATS', by Wanda Gag
'NOTHING BUT CATS', by Grace Skaar (World's Work)

## Acting-out ideas

'Three Little Kittens' (THE BOOK OF A THOUSAND POEMS)
'Where Are You Going To, My Pretty Maid?' and 'This is the house that Jack built' (THE PUFFIN BOOK OF NURSERY RHYMES)
'I do like a little bit of butter for my bread', from WHEN WE WERE VERY YOUNG, by A. A. Milne

These nursery rhymes and stories are good for dressing up and play acting. Try adapting nursery rhymes and stories for puppet shows when the children need something to start them off. (If you expect the children to say their lines right, you may all end up bad tempered. Interpret 'play acting' as 'playing at acting'.)

## TO INVESTIGATE

### Nature study

Place a horse chestnut twig with sticky buds in a glass of water. Each day the leaves will unfurl a little, opening like umbrellas. Look for the horseshoe-shaped marks where leaves have broken off the stem.

Look on rose bushes for rose-hips in the last stages of dehydration. Open one and look at the seeds.

## TO CREATE

### Furry pussy

Pussy willows begin sprouting this month. The children can gather pussy willow catkins, and then glue them inside the sketched outline of a cat to give it a furry textured coat.

### Thumbthings

Let the children ink their thumbs on a stamp pad, then make prints. Encourage them to use their imaginations to turn the prints into imaginary creatures.

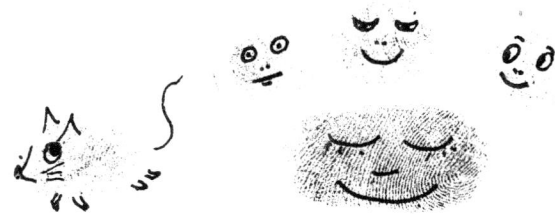

## TO FOLLOW UP

### A singing bird

This is a simple animation for you to show to the children.

You will need a note pad. Place it obliquely on the table in front of you so that one of the bottom corners is towards you. Draw a simple bird in a nest as shown. Go over the outline heavily so that you can trace it on the next page.

Add outstretched wings and a wide open beak to the traced outline on the second page. Go back to your first drawing. Starting at the corner, roll the page firmly over your pencil to half-way. Remove pencil. Use it to flip the curved paper back and forth over the second drawing. The bird will seem to raise its wings and open its beak.

# APRIL

## week 1

## TO TALK ABOUT

April brings sunshine, showers, Easter eggs, hot cross buns, spring rebirth, holidays, church services.

## TO LOOK FOR

### Green for the colour table

There is lots of green about this month.

Spring is here
Green shoots appear
In the ground
On the trees
All around.
                I.C.

Green is the traffic light colour for 'go'. Children can be confused about whether this means 'go' for them, or 'go' for the cars. Show them how the system works when you take them for walks. Never let under-fives cross streets alone. They are not ready for it, and drivers are not ready for them.

When you are out with the children, count how many green doors you pass, how many green buses you see, how many cats have green eyes. You might like to start a set of colour scrapbooks. To make your scrapbooks, fold sheets of stiff paper in half and place one on top of another, opened out. Make two holes on the fold and thread string through them. You can make the books as thick or as thin as you like. The children could sort through magazines for interesting green pictures to paste in the green book this month.

## TO JOIN IN

### Movement

Let the children pretend to be new spring shoots, pushing up through the earth. They begin sitting cross-legged on the floor, heads down—place palms of hands together and push them above heads—gradually stand and unfurl arms like flower petals. Now pretend a wind has sprung up, making the flowers sway and swing. Here comes a stronger wind with a whoosh, whirling the flowers right round and blowing them all over the room.

Away goes the wind and the children gently settle down on the floor for a rest.

### Action song

'Ten Green Bottles' (see October, week 3)

Humpty dumpty sat on a wall, (children sit or stand
                                        on chairs)
Humpty dumpty had a great fall, (all jump down and
                                        fall on floor)
All the king's horses and all the king's men,
Couldn't put Humpty together again. (as you pat
    each child to 'mend' him, he goes back to his chair)

### Nursery song

Hot cross buns, hot cross buns,
One a penny, two a penny, hot cross buns.
If you have no daughters,
Give them to your sons.
One a penny, two a penny, hot cross buns.

(Music in THE OXFORD NURSERY SONG BOOK)

## TO INVESTIGATE

### Milking a coconut

Imported coconuts appear in the shops this month. At one end of the coconut there is a monkey face. Push holes through the two eyes and the mouth. The shell here is thin, although the rest of the shell is very hard indeed. Now pour out the coconut milk.

You will have to split the coconut with a hammer and chisel to reach the nutty white flesh inside, which has to be prised from the shell in lumps. When the children have had enough to chew, put the rest out on the shell for the birds.

## Sound effects

Two half coconut shells can make a sound like a galloping horse's hooves.

## TO CREATE

### A coconut money box

See 'Things for adults to make'.

### Egg heads

To prepare the eggs, make a hole with a large needle at both ends, then blow out the contents, keeping the shell intact. Alternatively, you can hard-boil eggs so that they last indefinitely.

Stand each egg in an egg-cup for a child to draw a face. Felt-tip pens are good for this. Provide different kinds of 'hair' to glue on. Orange-red coloured medicated wadding makes a change from white cottonwool. Children can cut endless hat shapes out of paper pulp and plastic egg boxes.

### Tulips and mobiles

When you next eat boiled eggs, save the shells and wash them. Make a needle hole in the bottom of each and draw a thread through, fixing inside with a button or piece of matchstick. The children can dip the eggshells in vegetable dyes, or paint them. Tie the threads to a coathanger and you have a mobile. The children can glue on glitter when the shells have dried.

Gently ease eggshell 'tulips', or cut-up egg box cups, onto pipe cleaner stems. Dip into paint. Stand in a vase to dry.

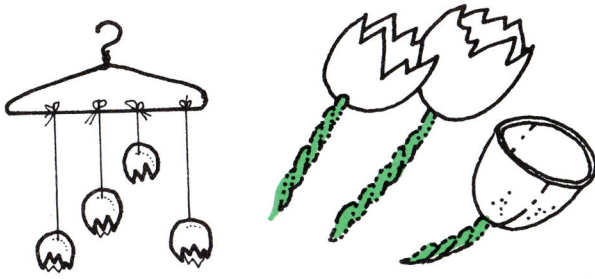

## Easter baskets

Make Easter egg baskets by stapling ribbon handles to plastic mousse or yogurt containers. Fill with cottonwool, clean wood shavings or stranded paper packing as a nest for a few small sugar or chocolate eggs.

**Make eggs** out of marzipan or fondant. (Marzipan recipe, October, week 4)

## TO FOLLOW UP

### Coloured Easter eggs

To colour eggs for Easter, first boil them, then place in a cup of hot water containing 1 dessertspoon of vinegar and 1 teaspoon of vegetable dye.

To initial eggs draw the first letter of the child's name on the eggshell with melted candle wax. When the wax has dried, soak the egg in vinegar for thirty minutes. Boil the egg in water to which vegetable dye has been added.

### The yolk of the year

This joke never fails. Blow an egg, so that you have an intact empty eggshell. Let the children place this in daddy's egg-cup at breakfast time. Serve the egg yolk and white cooked in some other way.

### Mosaics

1 The children break washed eggshells into small pieces.
2 You pour different coloured vegetable dyes into saucers. Very little is needed.
3 The children sprinkle the eggshells onto the saucers to soak up the colour, which it does in a very attractive way. Eggshells can also be painted with ordinary paint before breaking.
4 The children make a shape with glue on disposable paper plates.
5 Sprinkle on the eggshells. Glitter can be added for interest. The result is a framed mosaic picture.

### At home

Children enjoy the excitement of preparing a straw nest in a box for their Easter eggs to be laid in overnight.

## TO TALK ABOUT

### Easter by the sea

Are any of the children going to the seaside for a holiday this year? How many of them have ever seen the sea? Can they tell you what colour it is? It may be white with foam at the edges. It may look blue on a clear day, or grey on an overcast day, reflecting the sky. If water is very, very deep it usually looks green. But if you scoop a little water out of the sea, it is colourless, like tap water.

What sort of things does one find at the seaside? Maybe children could bring shells and other seaside treasures from home to show. Those lucky enough to be visiting the seaside could bring fresh treasures back. The Ladybird BOOK OF THE SEASHORE gives good object identification. It is even more useful if you jot the names of things shown on the illustration, so that you don't have to keep referring to the text. Another useful book that shows things to make is SEASIDE TREASURES (Mills and Boon).

## TO LOOK FOR

### Fruit in the shops now

Apples, oranges, apricots, melons, coconuts

## TO JOIN IN

### Movement

Imagine that you are all about to go paddling at the seaside. The children had better pretend to take off their shoes and socks. Walk out a little way, then a little bit further, to meet the sea. Run back quickly as a wave comes swooping in. Try walking sideways like a crab.

### Poem

'The Jumblies' (They went to sea in a sieve), by Edward Lear in THE COMPLETE NONSENSE OF EDWARD LEAR (Faber & Faber).

Experiment with a sieve or a colander in the water tray.

### Songs

A sailor went to sea, sea, sea, (salute three times)

To see what he could see, see, see. (shade eyes with hand three times)
But all that he could see, see, see, (shade eyes with hand three times)
Was sea, sea, sea. (salute three times)

The bear went over the mountain,
The bear went over the mountain,
The bear went over the mountain,
To see what he could see.
And all that he could see,
And all that he could see,
Was the other side of the mountain,
The other side of the mountain,
The other side of the mountain,
Was all that he could see!

Tongue-twister: She sells sea shells by the seashore.

## TO INVESTIGATE

### A seaside collection

Keep all your seaside treasures—shells, seaweed, small pieces of driftwood, etc.—in a large, strong box. Use them for sorting games, mosaics, montages, sand gardens, sticking into plasticine inside jar lids.

### A shell chart

Glue a specimen of each type of shell to the bottom of a shallow cardboard box. Label each specimen. Hang this on the wall or keep it on the nature table for a while. Put the lid back on the box and store it until you want to add to it, or refer to it again.

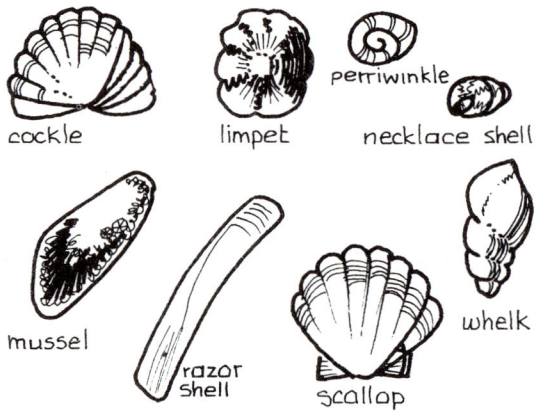

cockle    limpet    periwinkle    necklace shell    mussel    razor shell    scallop    whelk

## A necklace

Some shells have small holes in them. Usually this hole has been made by a tiny sea creature that is able to bore into the shell and eat the shellfish. Sometimes holes are made in shells when the sea washes them against rocks. It is almost impossible to make a hole in a shell without breaking it. But the children can thread the ones with holes already in, even if the hole is very broken away.

## Make it shine

Some shells, like the necklace shell, are pearlised inside. If you leave them to soak in vinegar, which is a mild acid, some of the lime which forms on the outside of the shell will dissolve. As some shells are thinner than others, check often to make sure the acid has not eaten too far. Now, with a wash and a rub, the whole shell will shine.

## TO CREATE

### Paperweights

Ask the children to look for large stones worn smooth by the sea. These make good paperweights. They may find one that has an unusual shape, one that is completely rounded, or one that has colour in it. A coat of varnish will capture the watery shine. Children might want to paint stones or glue shells all around before varnishing. Small pebbles all about the same size could be glued on a piece of board to make a heat-resistant stand for hot saucepans.

### Shell pots and plaques

Coat the outside of plastic yogurt pots with plaster of paris or cellulose filler (Polyfilla). The children can press in shells while the coating is still wet. Varnish. Shells look very attractive when children have arranged and stuck them on a flat board. If you drill a hole in the board before applying plaster or glue, it can be hung on the wall. Children can glue shells on interesting pieces of driftwood for room ornaments. They can bind shells together with strong glue, clay, or plaster to make funny people and animals.

Mix plaster of paris in a plastic bowl. Unused plaster should be left to set hard in bowl, then chipped out and thrown in dustbin. Rinsing it down the sink will clog your drains.

### An undersea frieze

Let the children glue all the remaining treasures they have brought from the seaside on a long strip of paper that will stretch along one wall. Paint in a few wavy lines and bubbles to give the effect of looking through water.

### Counting with shells

Cut large numbers out of thin cardboard or stiff paper. Help the children to glue the appropriate number of shells on each number.

Shells can be sorted into bun trays. How many small shells fit into a bun shape? How many large shells fit into the same shape?

### Super sorting game

Take a large cardboard grocery carton. Open it out flat. Draw a large circle in the middle with paths leading to smaller circles. Place a mixture of different kinds of things in the centre circle; for example, buttons, shells, pebbles and milk bottle tops. Place one of each kind of thing in each small circle. The children can sit around the carton on the floor and sort the things in the big circle into the appropriate small circles. This works equally well with different kinds of shells, different regiments of toy soldiers, different farm animals, or different coloured toy cars. It opens up lots of opportunity for discovery and comparison, which is at least as important as the actual sorting. You can place a farmhouse or garage in the middle when the sorting has been done, leading to imaginative play.

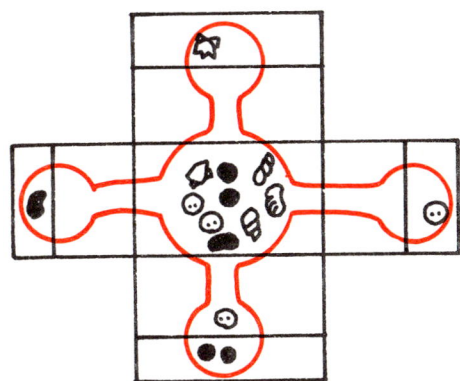

### Listen to the sea

Hold a large shell to a child's ear so she can 'hear the sea' in it. Demonstrate with a very large shell to toddlers who might poke tiny shells inside their ears.

### Sand angels

Lie flat on dry sand. Move arms up and down, legs sideways, to make an imprint of an angel with wings and a wide skirt.

### A sand garden

Smooth a small area of sand flat. Make shell borders, plant seaweed hedges. Let imagination take over.

# APRIL

# week 3

## TO TALK ABOUT

### Spring awakening

The chickens and baby rabbits we think of at Easter are very much in evidence now in the country. In gardens, dragonflies and other insects are hatching from the cocoons that have protected them all winter. Many new caterpillars will be looking for food to eat, and birds will be looking for them, to feed their own young. If the children find a chrysalis on a bush in the garden and want to see what it hatches into, tie part of an old nylon stocking around it on the twig, and check daily.

Save clear plastic bottles. Cut off both ends. Wrap net around the ends with a draw-string top. You can keep unhatched insect specimens in these, tied to a tree or a wire coat-hanger hooked up outdoors. This is better than keeping them in bottles indoors, unless they are varieties that need a constant high temperature, because their natural environment is best and many need rain to help them develop fully. This way, rain will drain through naturally. Of course, once examined, living creatures should be set free. Choose a place where they will not be spotted easily by birds. We should be able to enjoy the beauty of, say, a dragonfly without feeling the need to capture it.

## TO LOOK FOR

### Plant life

Daisies, cowslips, germander speedwell, dandelions (blow away the hours on these thistle 'fairy clocks'), buttercups, magnolia, forget-me-not, veronica, gorse. Flowers appear on oak trees. The blackthorn tree is white with flowers and the flowering cherry has pink blooms. The yellow flowers of the laburnum tree are budding. (Warn children that laburnum seeds are poisonous and repeat the warning later in the year when the pods appear.)

Pick 'honesty' now and hang it upside down until September. Then the outer leaves can be removed and the seeds saved. Use the silvery centres still on the stem to brighten up a room.

## TO JOIN IN

### Action songs

1, 2, 3, 4, 5
Once I caught a fish alive.
6, 7, 8, 9, 10
Then I let him go again.
Why did you let him go?
Because he bit my finger so.
Which finger did he bite?
This little finger on the right.

Try dividing the children into two singing groups, each led by an adult. The first group sings the first line; the second group sings the second line and so on.

Wriggle your fingers and hands to and fro like fish swimming for:

Down in the meadow in an itty bitty pool,
Lived three little fishes and a mummy fishy too.
Swim, said the mother fishy, swim if you can,
And they swam and they swam all over the dam.

(on record, CHILDREN'S FAVOURITES MFP1175)

### Rhymes

'Over in the meadow in the sand in the sun' from ONE, TWO, BUCKLE MY SHOE (World's Work)

Four and twenty tailors went to catch a snail,
Not one man among them durst touch her tail,
She put out her horns like a little Kyloe cow,
Run, tailors, run, or she'll have you all e'en now.

The cuckoo comes in April,
Sings a song in May,
In the middle of June another tune,
And then he flies away.

## TO INVESTIGATE

### Magnetic attraction

Put out magnets for the children to experiment with. Explain how two magnets attract or repel one another. Move one magnet about on top of a piece of cardboard by moving another magnet below. Make it 'jump' by inverting the bottom magnet so that it repels the top one.

Let children pass magnets over a box of odds and ends to see what is picked up. Let them try lots of things to see what responds to magnetic attraction, and what does not. (Not all metals are attracted.)

## TO CREATE

### A fishing game

Under adult supervision 4–5-year-olds can be helped to saw lengths of balsa wood into medium size pieces. Real tools in the smallest size are best, but must be strictly supervised. Use a vice to hold the wood and explain how the fingers are always placed well away from the cutting edge. Next, hammer a brass tack into one end of each piece. Paint on a fish shape, or stick on circles of coloured gummed paper for scales, eyes and mouth. Tie magnets on string onto stick fishing rods and have fun catching the fish. More than two anglers at a time in a small area can lead to an awful confusion of lines and magnets.

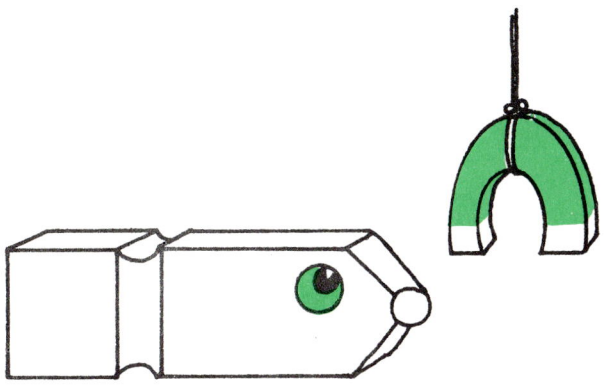

If the fish are made by an adult, the balsa wood can easily be carved into a fish shape. If painted with gold and silver enamel paint, they can be put into a basin of water, which adds a lot of fun to the game.

### A fish montage

Draw a big, fat fish shape on a large sheet of paper. Have a supply of milk bottle tops saved for scales, or use circles cut from aluminium foil. How many milk bottle tops do the children think you will need to fill in this shape? A few or a lot? Glue on a few. Now, how many more do the children think you need to glue on? A few more? A lot more? Draw a medium-sized fish and a small fish. Do the children think you will need more or less bottle tops to fill in these shapes than you will need for the large fish? Divide your supply of bottle tops into three heaps, large, medium and small, and see how close your guess was to the amount needed.

The children can help to stick bottle tops on your drawings, or they can make their own pictures of whatever they like, using 'scale' shapes—circles of cloth, gummed paper, silver foil, coloured cellophane, or milk bottle tops, and buttons.

You can make a fish that reflects light by cutting the overall shape out of silver foil, and gluing on coloured cellophane scales. What happens where two transparent colours overlap? The shade changes! Can anybody bring a real goldfish in a tank for the children to observe?

## TO FOLLOW UP

### Track down snails

Have the children noticed the silvery trail snails leave wherever they pass? Snails lay their own tracks for their smooth legless bodies to glide along. This track is strong enough to make a bridge over a corrugated surface, smoothing out the ridges. If you put a snail in a bottle with a piece of lettuce, the children will be able to watch its undulating movement as it glides up the glass. If you put the bottle outside, the snail will soon find its way out and back to some shady corner of the garden.

### Worms

Look for worms. You should find them quite near the surface of the moist earth, waiting for April showers. Worms are useful things to have in a garden because their holes aerate the soil. Birds will be looking for worms to feed their young. Fish like worms, too.

### 'Flip the kipper'

Cut some fish shapes out of newspaper. Roll up old magazines and sticky-tape them to make batons. The children kneel at one end of a long rug. They must try to flip the paper fish to the opposite end by whacking the floor with the batons to create a breeze.

## TO TALK ABOUT

### Boats

Good boating weather begins in April. You are likely to see rowing teams training on main rivers. You might see small rowing boats at the seaside. Have the children noticed how an oar seems to bend where it breaks the surface of the water? If you hold a stick straight down in the water tray, you will see the same effect. Ruffle the water and the stick seems to wriggle.

## TO LOOK FOR

### Wildlife

Hedgehogs are awake after hibernation, and feeding. Look for a hawk, first cuckoo, redstart.

### Weather

Sunshine, showers, thunderstorms. Check your thermometer. Has the mercury risen since last month? Sometimes there is a late snap of very cold weather in April.

## TO JOIN IN

### Movement

The children can sit in two rows on the floor and pretend to be rowing in a boat race. It will soon become obvious why it is important for everyone to pull in the same direction at the same time. Now the children can choose partners. Face partners sitting on the floor with feet touching. Clasp each other's hands. Rock back and forth as if rowing, and sing to the rhythm.

### Rowing Songs

Row, row, row your boat
Gently down the stream.
Merrily, merrily, merrily, merrily,
Life is but a dream.

(Music in THIS LITTLE PUFFIN)

The big ship sails on the Alley, Alley-O,
    the Alley, Alley-O,
    the Alley, Alley-O.

The big ship sails on the Alley, Alley-O,
On the first day of September.
Verse 2: The big ship sails to the bottom of the sea.

(Music in THIS LITTLE PUFFIN)

What shall we do with a drunken sailor?
What shall we do with a drunken sailor?
What shall we do with a drunken sailor?
Early in the morning?
Verse 2: Put him in a tub and wash him all over.

Michael, row the boat ashore,
Alleluya!
Michael, row the boat ashore,
Alleluya!

Next verses:
(child's name) help to trim the sails . . .
(child's name) hold the rudder straight . . .
(child's name) bail the water out . . .
(child's name) look out for the shore . . .
(child's name) let the anchor down . . .

Notice how the strong beats in sea shanties give you a rowing rhythm, so you all can pull together. Try keeping the beat with hand clapping, then instruments.

### Nursery rhymes

Have the children ever seen well-buckets working on a pulley? 'Jack and Jill went up the hill to fetch a pail of water' (PUFFIN BOOK OF NURSERY RHYMES) is a rhyme that little children of long ago might have made up as they pulled hand over hand on the rope to bring the water up out of the well.

Can you and the children think of any other rhymes or songs that seem to have action in the rhythm? 'See-saw, Marjorie Daw' is one.

That old favourite song, 'There's a hole in my bucket', is on Hallmark Record HMA 245, GROWING UP WITH WALLY WHYTON.

## TO INVESTIGATE

### Reflections

Can any of the children remember having seen trees,

buildings or their own faces reflected in the water of a stream, pond or puddle? If you can take the children with safety to a nearby waterhole, look for reflections; drop a stone in and see how the water ripples outwards in ever-increasing circles; skim a flat stone over the surface of the water. Take a newspaper boat to sail.

Have the children ever thrown a penny into a 'magic' fountain or wishing well? What thoughts occur to them about water?

## April celebrations

Queen's birthday; anniversary of St Anselm, protector of wishing wells, fountains and springs; St George's day. Do the children know of any statues of St George killing a fierce dragon? There might be a St George stained glass window in your local church.

## TO CREATE

### Ships

See how many different kinds of ship you can make out of junk material. Take it slowly. Make it a joint effort with suggestions from everybody who is interested. Use pictures for reference. A liner has funnels and is large. A viking boat is narrow and long, but not as long as a liner, and has lots of oars. A sailing ship is tall with mast and sail. It might be taller than a liner, but not as long and wide. What different kinds of power did these ships use to move over the water? How about a paddle steamer and a submarine? Give the children a chance to make their own creations out of junk, clay or plasticine.

## TO FOLLOW UP

### Water play

Play a game of guessing which objects will sink and which will float, before the children put them to the test in the water tray.

Drinking-straws float because air is trapped in the middle. You can make a raft by gluing and binding straws together. You can make another raft by soaking wood spills and weaving them together. Now you can float a stone on top. Gentle splashing at one end of the tray will create a current that will help move the raft along.

The children can make bubbles by blowing air out of a straw under water. Syphon water out by placing a finger over the end of the straw to create suction. Experiment with an eye-dropper.

The children are discovering these things for themselves every day at waterplay. They will appreciate your interest and the chance to talk about what they are doing, leading to fresh avenues of discovery.

Halves of walnut shells make good boats. Add a matchstick mast, held in place with plasticine, and a paper sail. In July try this with pea-pods available then.

## A paper boat

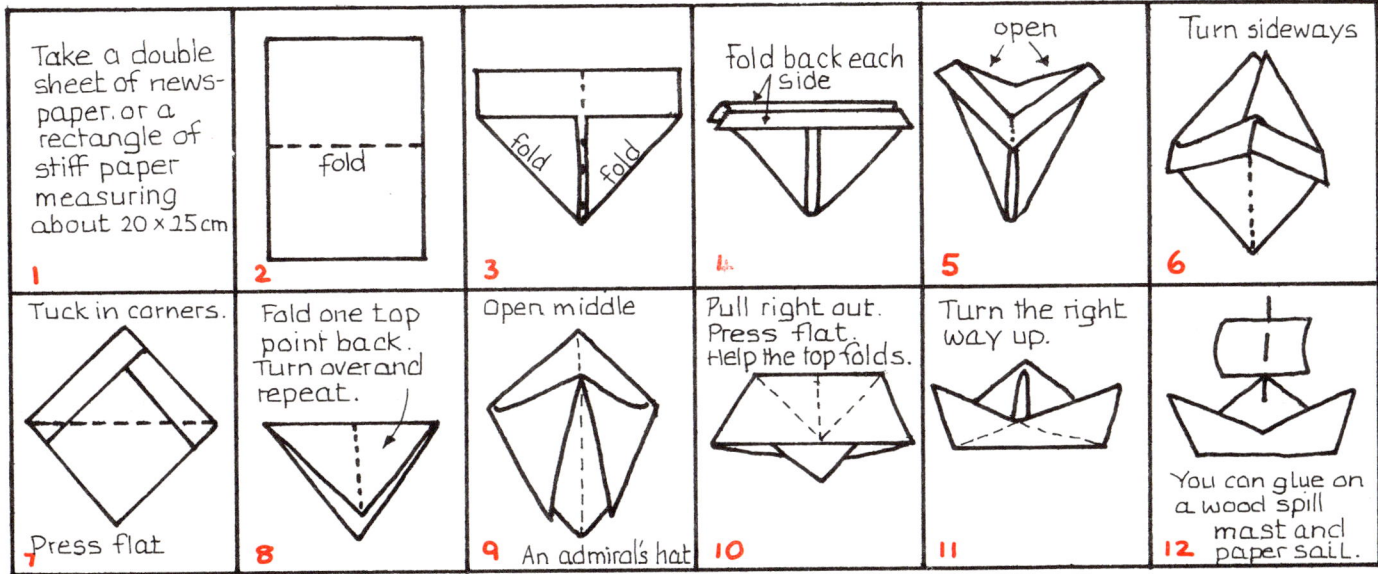

1. Take a double sheet of newspaper, or a rectangle of stiff paper measuring about 20 × 25 cm
2. fold
3. fold fold
4. Fold back each side
5. open
6. Turn sideways
7. Tuck in corners. Press flat
8. Fold one top point back. Turn over and repeat.
9. Open middle. An admiral's hat
10. Pull right out. Press flat. Help the top folds.
11. Turn the right way up.
12. You can glue on a wood spill mast and paper sail.

# MAY

# week 1

## TO TALK ABOUT

### May Day

Everybody feels like celebrating the beginning of May because summer seems just around the corner. Many countries hold May Day parades or processions down main streets on May 1. Sometimes a 'Queen of the May' is chosen. In England Morris dancers give their traditional performances. People dance around Maypoles on village greens.

## TO LOOK FOR

### Blue for the colour table

Blue is a primary colour. Blue and yellow make green. Blue is the colour of the May sky much of the time. Look for May bluebells. Blue comes in bright shades, but it is generally a soft colour.

### All the colours of the rainbow

If you refract the sun's rays through a glass prism, you can see all the rainbow colours. There are seven altogether—red, orange, yellow, green, blue, indigo, violet. Sometimes you can see them in a bubble, or deflected off the bevelled edge of a mirror.

The rainbow we sometimes see in the sky after rain is caused by the sunlight being refracted by raindrops.

## TO JOIN IN

### Songs

All clap hands to:

The animals went in two by two, hurrah, hurrah,
The animals went in two by two, hurrah, hurrah,
The animals went in two by two, the elephant and the
   kangaroo,
They all went into the ark for to get out of the rain.
Verse 2:
The insects went in three by three,
The butterfly, ant and bumble bee . . .
Verse 3:
The birds came flying in four by four,
Then old Noah shut the door,
When they'd all gone into the ark for to get out of
   the rain.

Tune 'When Johnny comes marching home', in THE OXFORD NURSERY SONG BOOK.

Another 'Noah' song, 'One more river to cross' is also in THE OXFORD NURSERY SONG BOOK.

'Who built the ark? Noah, Noah!' can be found in AMERICAN FOLK SONGS FOR CHILDREN, collected by Ruth Crawford Seeger.

### Poem

*Raindrops and Sunbeams*

A million little diamonds
Sparkled on the trees,
And all the little maidens said,
'A jewel if you please.'
But whilst they stood with arms outstretched
To catch the jewels gay,
A million little sunbeams came
And stole them all away.
         (Poet unknown)

## TO INVESTIGATE

### The legendary crock of gold

Have any of the children seen a rainbow recently? There is a saying that there is a crock, or pot, of gold at the end of the rainbow. The trouble is that the rainbow always seems to end a long way away, or nowhere at all, just fading from view.

### Noah's Ark

The Old Testament tells us that long, long ago there was a great flood over all the earth. It rained and rained until the ground was completely covered with water. Noah had been warned of this by God and so he collected two of every kind of animal. He built a large houseboat, called an ark, and all his family and the animals sailed around in it until the water went down and they could walk on dry land again. When the rain stopped, God created the rainbow as a sign of peace to Noah.

### The 'ole in the ark

There is an old, funny story that the ark sprang a leak. It was just a tiny hole at first. To stop the water coming through, the dog poked his nose in the hole. That's why dogs always have cold noses.

The hole became bigger so Mrs Noah put her elbow in it. Now ladies often have cold elbows. The hole finally became so big that Mr Noah had to sit on it. And that, they say, is why men always stand with their backs to the fire. (To warm their cold bottoms.)

## TO CREATE

### A rainbow

Let the children paint their own rainbows, trying to use the colours in the correct order. They may be more successful with crayons, over which they have greater control. They might graduate to making a picture with a rainbow in it. Encourage them to express some little thought about a rainbow, which you can print on the picture as the simplest kind of prose poem.

## TO FOLLOW UP

### Your own personal rainbow

You can make a rainbow with the aid of a mirror on a sunny day. Take an open, shallow tray like a baking tin. Half-fill it with water. Place a pocket mirror half in the water, slanting it with a ball of plasticine behind. When a shaft of sunlight catches the mirror, it will deflect a rainbow onto the nearest surface—wall or child. If you peer into the mirror below the water line, you will see a rainbow around your face. Place the baking tin on a chair and move it around the garden to keep catching the sun.

### Rainbow bubbles

Have a bubble-blowing session. Look at the rainbow colours captured in each bubble.

To make a good bubble-blowing mixture soak slivers of soap overnight in a little water. Liquid detergent is not so suitable for young children, who are likely to swallow some of the liquid.

If children are using bubble pipes rather than

wands, show them how to hold the pipe upside down when they dip it in the soap bowl. That way they are less likely to have soapy water from the pipe bowl running into their mouths and bubbles popping in their faces.

### Sunbeams and secret signals

Have the children noticed how on cloudy days the sun shines between breaks in the clouds in little shafts? Sometimes the rays shine through branches of trees in this way or through chinks in the curtains if they are drawn. It is interesting to watch because you can see all the dust that is about us all the time, floating up and down the ray of light.

If a mirror or any other shiny surface catches the sun, it glints and gleams and can reflect a very bright light onto a nearby wall. The light can be made to dance all around the room by moving the object. It looks like a sun fairy.

You can make flashes by using a shiny object to reflect the sun. The flashes could be used for sending a secret signal to someone watching from a long way away. When the children try this, warn them not to shine a light directly in anyone's eyes. The sun should not be looked at directly.

## TO TALK ABOUT

### Hush-a-bye baby

In May you can't help hearing the birds singing their welcome to the coming summer. Their nests bob up and down on the windswept branches of trees. 'Hush-a-bye baby on the tree-top' might have been written about a baby bird in a nest.

Do any of the children have eiderdowns on their beds at home? The very soft, warm feathers for this come from the breast of the eider duck, who uses them to feather her own nest.

## TO LOOK FOR

### Fruit in the shops now

Apricots, gooseberries, rhubarb

## TO JOIN IN

### Movement

The children hold hands and skip around in a ring for,

Here we come gathering nuts in May,
Nuts in May, nuts in May.
Here we come gathering nuts in May,
On a cold and frosty morning.

Continue with any things children would normally do before going to gather nuts in May, such as,

This is the way we get out of bed,
Get out of bed, get out of bed.
This is the way we get out of bed,
On a cold and frosty morning.

(Repeat chorus)

Don't forget the actions for 'clean our teeth', 'wash our face', etc.

(Music in THE OXFORD NURSERY SONG BOOK)

### Rhymes

Hush-a-bye baby,
On the tree top.
When the wind blows,
The cradle will rock.
When the bough breaks,
The cradle will fall—
And down will come baby,
Cradle and all.
(Music in THE OXFORD NURSERY SONG BOOK)

I saw a little bird come hop, hop, hop,
And I said, little bird, will you stop, stop, stop?
I was going to the window,
To say, 'how do you do?'
When he shook his little head,
And away he flew.

## TO INVESTIGATE

### Wise words about May weather

Children are especially at risk for catching colds in May. The days seem sunny and, after the dull winter, children are only too eager to run out of doors in light clothing. Back up your arguments for keeping coats on a little longer with this age-old advice:

'Cast ne'er a clout 'till May be out'

and

'Said the wise man to his son,
Keep on thy coat 'till May is done.'

and

'If you would the doctor pay,
Leave your flannels off in May!'

Once upon a time children were sewn into their warm flannel underwear so that they wouldn't catch cold. Imagine not taking a bath all winter!

### Saying and doing

Do the children know the saying, 'as light as a feather'? Let them throw feathers up in the air to see how softly and lightly they float down. Try weighing some feathers on scales. Make a game of trying to keep a feather afloat by blowing.

## TO CREATE

### An Indian headdress

Collect pigeon or seagull feathers. Let the children paint them bright colours. Allow a day to dry.

Cut corrugated cardboard into strips about 4 cm

(1½″) wide and 1 metre long, or head-size if you are short of feathers. Stick feathers in at regular intervals. Stick a strip of sticky tape along the back of the cardboard and along the bottom of the feathers, to hold them in place. Fit around the child's head and fasten with a paperclip. Fasten the trailing ends together with another paperclip.

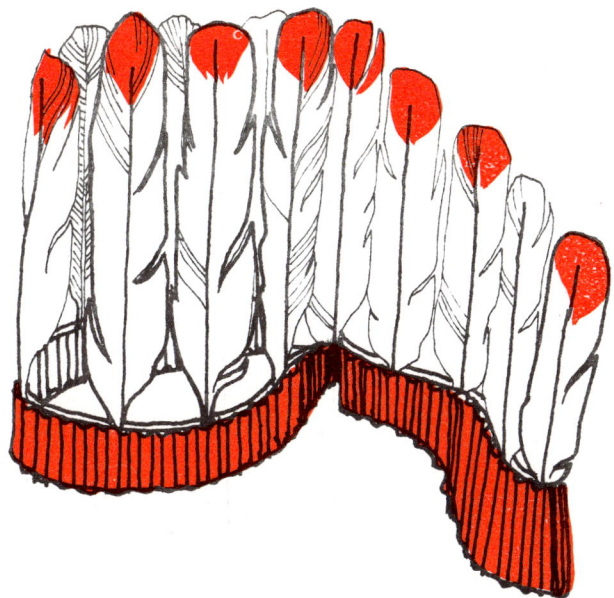

Old curtains draped over a clothes line, swing frame or table will make an Indian tent. Clothes pegs will help to keep the curtains in place.

## A paper fold glider

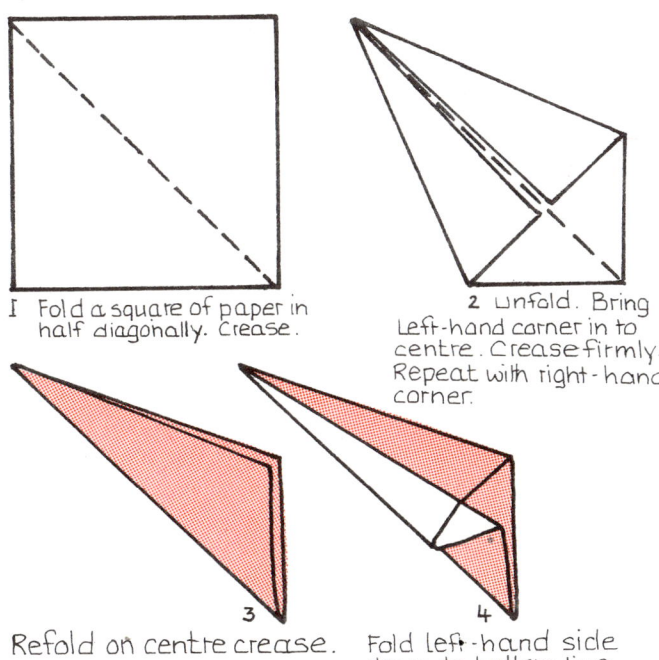

1 Fold a square of paper in half diagonally. Crease.

2 Unfold. Bring left-hand corner in to centre. Crease firmly. Repeat with right-hand corner.

3 Refold on centre crease.

4 Fold left-hand side down to bottom line. Crease.

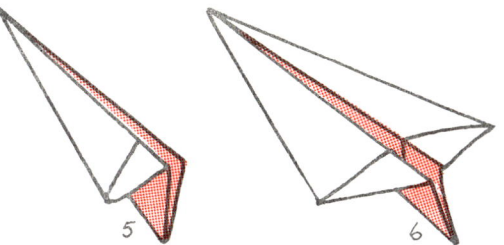

5 Turn model over. Fold right-hand side down.

6 Your glider is ready to fly. Test which way the wind is blowing before you launch it.

## TO FOLLOW UP

### Interesting facts about feathers

Bird feathers are useful and ornamental. Can the children think of ways in which feathers help birds? They keep the birds warm, they help them to fly, they make them look attractive to their mates.

Can the children think of ways in which feathers help people? They keep us warm in eiderdowns. They help us to sleep, in soft pillows. They are sometimes worn on hats, to look attractive.

Ostrich plumes are sometimes worn on the hats of Heads of State, as an indication of the man's importance. American Indians used eagle feathers for headdresses. New Zealand Maoris wear kiwi feather cloaks as part of their national costume. The Australian emu has feathers, but is too large to fly. The lyre-bird has a tail shaped just like a lyre, a harp-like musical instrument. The peacock has a tail like a beautiful fan. He spreads it, shakes it, then folds it again. He struts about, looking very proud of his fine feathers . . . 'as proud as a peacock'. Have any of the children seen a peacock spread his magnificent tail? Peacocks shed some of their tail feathers at certain times of the year. A zoo may be happy to let you have one or two, if you inquire at the office and they have some to spare.

Goose feathers were used in bygone days for quill pens. The children could try making marks with a feather. Split the end and dip it in ink or paint.

### 'Does it fly?'

The leader calls out the names of different animals, birds, insects, anything that comes to mind. The children concentrate. Whenever the leader mentions something that flies, the children should put their arms out like wings. There are bound to be lots of funny guesses. This provides opportunity for fun and fact-finding.

### A singing bird

See March, week 4

### Look at

DO YOU KNOW ABOUT FEATHERS?, by Kathleen A. Shoesmith (Burke)

## TO TALK ABOUT

### Fossils

The bodies of many sea creatures that lived long ago, especially urchins and shellfish, became embedded in lime and turned into fossils. Extinct land animals left behind fossilised bones, which give us an idea of what they must have looked like. Sometimes they left no more than their footprints in soft clay that hardened over the centuries.

Many of these relics are discovered in limestone cliffs at the seaside. You might even find a stone with a piece of fossilised bone in it in your garden.

Perhaps you could take the children to see some reconstructed prehistoric animals at a museum. Can anybody bring an ammonite or other fossil, or an insect in amber for the children to look at?

Pictures in books will be popular. Seeing enormous animals that are extinct and no longer a threat gives children a satisfying sense of power.

### Everybody's bones

Explain to the children that we have bones inside us, just as the animals do. Have any of the children ever had an X-ray taken of their bones or their teeth?

Perhaps a hospital will let you have an old X-ray plate to look at. Understanding what happens could save a child anxiety if an X-ray were needed in an emergency.

## TO LOOK FOR

### Plant life

Hawthorn blossom (also called May), smell the perfume; wild hyacinth (bluebell), flowering broom shrub, wallflower, pink campion, cuckoo-pint (the scarlet berries that appear in autumn are poisonous), tulips, lilac, bird's foot trefoil flowers. The horse chestnut is in bloom. Its flowers look like candles, and it is sometimes called 'the candle tree'.

## TO JOIN IN

### Movement

If your local library has a record section, you may be able to reserve CAMARATA (Carnival of the Animals), by C. Saint-Saëns, with verses by Ogden Nash. Act out the animal movements.

Do simple exercises on a mat to strengthen growing bones and keep them supple. 'Bicycling' flat out on the back with legs in the air is a favourite. The children pretend to be pedalling slowly up a hill. It is very hard work. Then their knees work faster and faster as the imaginary bicycle speeds down the other side of the hill.

### Action rhymes

I've got one head,
One nose, too.
One mouth, one chin,
So have you.

I've got two eyes,
Two ears, too.
Two arms, two legs,
And so have you.

I've got two hands,
Two thumbs too.
Four fingers on each hand—
And so have you.

Fingers, thumbs and toes,
Eyes and ears and nose,
Lips and chin, hair and skin,
Have you got all those?

Fingers, thumbs and toes,
Eyes and ears and nose,
Lips and chin, hair and skin,
YES! We have all those.

March winds,
April showers,
Bring forth,
May flowers.

How many days has my baby to play?
Saturday, Sunday, Monday,
Tuesday, Wednesday, Thursday, Friday,
Saturday, Sunday, Monday.

## Story

'The Tale of a Hazel Nut' from TELL ME A STORY, collected by Eileen Colwell (Puffin)

## TO INVESTIGATE

### Lenses

In the dark, shine a torch under a child's hand. It creates an illusion of being able to see through the edges of the fingers. Provide a torch for the children to take apart, so they can see how it works. Point out the magnifying lens, which enlarges the light from the tiny bulb. In the same way, the glass in a watch enlarges the tiny figures and makes them more easily readable.

Spectacles enlarge printed words. Spectacles can be a bit of a mystery to children. A clear explanation of their purpose, and some discussion, is helpful to those who don't wear glasses as well as to those who do.

Look at the beautiful glass flowers inside old paperweights. Look at real flowers through a magnifying glass.

## TO CREATE

### Clay play

Cut lengths of garden wire and twist them into armatures. These are the skeleton frames that form the bases for professionally modelled figures. The children can cover the skeletons with clay or plasticine to create monsters.

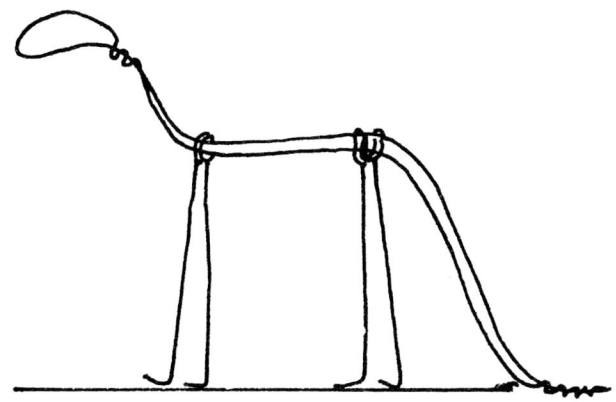

### A skeleton costume

For a child's fancy dress, combine an old black sweater with black tights. Paint on bones in white.

## TO FOLLOW UP

### Insects and plants

The children should be able to see plenty of butterflies and caterpillars about now, especially the common blue butterfly, whose caterpillars are found on bird's foot trefoil flowers. Insects have looked much the same for millions of years. We know this because many became trapped in the sap of trees. The sap hardened into amber with the insect fossilised inside.

Look at pine resin, plum-tree resin and other types of tree and plant sap. Snap a dandelion stem to see its white, sticky sap. Sap is the 'blood' of plants. With certain flowers, the end of the stems must be singed when they are picked, so that the sap doesn't drain away and cause the flower to die quickly.

### Look at

FOSSILS TELL OF LONG AGO, by Aliki (A. & C. Black)

## TO TALK ABOUT

### Wonders of the insect world

Have the children seen any wasps, hornets or bees about? These insects all have nasty stings so warn the children to leave them well alone. The homes of these insects should be given a wide berth. If an adult can find an abandoned or smoked-out wasp or hornet nest to bring to playgroup, the children will find the fluted structure, papery texture and distinctive shapes fascinating. A wax honeycomb is interesting too. These can be obtained from health food stores, and children will enjoy sampling some of the honey on cracker biscuits.

The radiator grill on some cars is like a honeycomb. The shape of each cell is hexagonal. A hexagon has six sides.

Everything in the insect world is very small, and very interesting, especially examined under a magnifying glass or microscope.

## TO LOOK FOR

### Wildlife

Tadpoles develop back legs. Birds are still nesting. The swallow, skylark, goldfinch, and bullfinch are to be seen. Listen for the nightingale. Insects abound.

### Weather

Some cold days still. Generally warm and windy. Check thermometer.

## TO JOIN IN

### Stories

'The Grasshopper and the Ants', from AESOP'S FABLES
The ANT AND BEE series
THE VERY HUNGRY CATERPILLAR, by Eric Carle (Hamish Hamilton)

### Nursery rhyme

Ladybird, ladybird, fly away home.
Your house is on fire, your children are gone.
All except one, whose name is Ann,
And she crept under the frying-pan.

'Who's that tickling my back?' said the wall.
'Me,' said a small caterpillar.
'I'm learning to crawl.'
Ian Serraillier

### Action rhyme

All buzz about like busy bees to:

Aeroplanes, aeroplanes, all in a row.
Aeroplanes, aeroplanes, ready to go.
Hark, they're beginning to buzz and to hum.
The engines are working, so come along, come.
Now we are flying right up in the sky.
Faster and faster—oh, ever so high.
Linda Chesterman

(Music in THIS LITTLE PUFFIN)

## TO INVESTIGATE

### Remedies for stings

If a child is unlucky enough to be stung by a bee, carefully remove the sting and poison sac intact, if possible. Use tweezers sterilised by boiling, or a needle passed through a flame and allowed to cool for a few seconds. If the poison sac is broken, the poison will have spread on the skin. Wash very carefully around the wound. Apply a wet blue-bag or other recommended ointment. There is a spray obtainable from chemists that anaesthetises the skin, reducing pain quickly.

If a child is stung by a nettle, rub on a dock leaf, squeezing out the juice. Where there are nettles, there are usually docks. Wet sand is also good for rubbing on stings if nothing else is available.

## TO CREATE

### Turn caterpillars into butterflies

Making a large butterfly with stiffened wings is too difficult for under-fives, but they can learn much from watching you make it. They can enjoy making floppy-winged butterflies and bees themselves.

You will need a bag of assorted balloons (make sure there are enough balloons for all the children), a balloon pump, two shades of coloured tissue paper, strong glue, clear sticky tape, pipe cleaners, garden wire, pliers, scissors, tape measure, black thread, a pencil, string, newspapers to protect the table top while you work with glue.

*Large butterfly*

1  Blow up a long balloon. From coloured tissue paper, cut out two large circles for eyes, and two smaller circles in a darker colour for pupils. Cut out a mouth. Glue in place, at the opposite end to the tying end of your balloon. That is your caterpillar. Put it to one side.

Look up a picture of a caterpillar in THE OXFORD BOOK OF INSECTS or a similar insect reference book from your local library. Show it to the children. Discuss its similarities to the balloon caterpillar, and its differences. What are its eyes really like? Does it have a mouth shaped like a human mouth? How many legs does it have?

2  Blow up a round balloon. This is the chrysalis stage. Put it to one side. Look at pictures in your reference book with the children. What are the similarities and what are the differences? What happens during this stage?

3  Measure 2 m (6'6") of garden wire. Cut it with pliers. Bend it to the shape of a pair of wings. Bind the two ends together in the middle with pliers. Explain to the children that you don't want to leave any sharp ends to scratch them or puncture the balloon. Place this shape on a folded sheet of coloured tissue paper. Draw around, leaving a good overlap. Cut out the two thicknesses.

Take one thickness. Glue well around the edges. Brush glue in streaks out from the centre of the wings, like the veins on a real butterfly's wings. Place the wire shape on the paper. Place the other thickness of paper over the top, and smooth down. Glue or sticky-tape this to the back of your original caterpillar. Sticky-tape pipe cleaners in place above eyes for antennae. Move your butterfly up and down to make the wings flap. Suspend it from the ceiling with a loop of black cotton thread fore and aft of the wings.

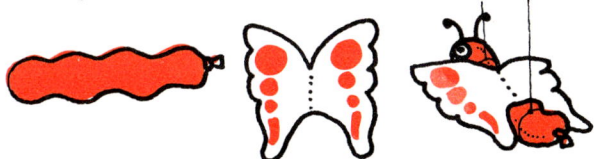

Look at pictures of real butterflies. Are your antennae in the right place? What are they for? How are the wings joined to the body? Are they veined like your glue veins?

*Floppy butterfly*

Blow up the rest of the balloons. Let the children cut wings out of a piece of coloured tissue paper, and

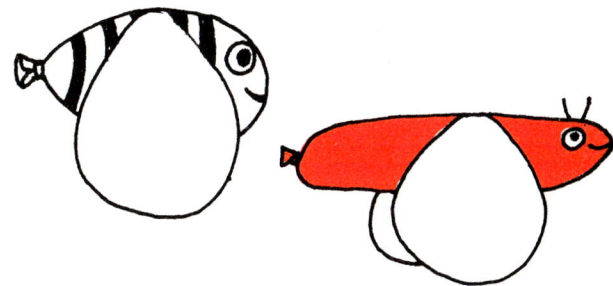

glue or sticky-tape them in place on a balloon. They can cut eyes and mouths out of remaining scraps of paper, and glue them on; sticky-tape antennae in place. The round balloons can be chrysalises or bees. At this stage you might find it wise to print each child's name under one wing of his or her creation, before they get mixed up. Have plenty of string on hand for tying to balloons.

Rub balloons on sweaters to create static electricity. They will then pick up all the little bits of tissue paper left over. See if the balloons will stick to the wall.

If the children are still in a creative mood, they can paint stripes on the bees, veins on the wings, markings on the caterpillars, splodges on chrysalises.

**A counting picture**

See 'Things for adults to make'

**TO FOLLOW UP**

**Bread and butter flowers**

This month you can sow nasturtium seeds, which will flower later in the summer. Bees sip nectar out of flowers for making honey. If you and the children would like to try some flower nectar, pick a nasturtium flower, nip the tip off the long tube at the back, and suck. The leaves of the nasturtium, when washed, can be eaten on bread and butter. They are rather bitter, so try just a little, finely chopped. Warn the children not to try tasting other kinds of flowers, as some, like the foxglove, are poisonous.

**Egg box caterpillar**

Cut out two rows of egg cups for each child to sticky-tape together. Add eyes and mouth, pipe-cleaner feelers and a little tail.

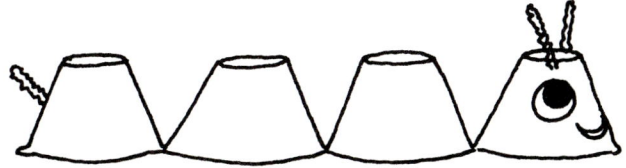

**Look at**

LADYBIRDS, SNAILS AND OTHER THINGS! by Althea (Dinosaur)

# JUNE week 1

## TO TALK ABOUT

### Flaming June

June is the sixth month of the year. As there are twelve months in a year, June and July come in the middle. You could make a list of the months of the year and underline June to show its position—a long way from and to Christmas.

June days can be very warm. This month is sometimes called 'flaming June' because of the heat, and maybe because gardens are ablaze with the colour of roses.

### Sets

What sets of things can you think of that can be illustrated? There are the seasons, the days of the week, the hours of the day. The children might like to paint things that they enjoy doing on different days of the week. Use their paintings and a few simple words, figures, or line drawings to chart these sets of things. Set them out logically on the wall, or a display board.

Other sets of things that can be illustrated are numbers 1 to 20, letters of the alphabet, and time—quarter past, half past, three-quarters of an hour, and an hour.

## TO LOOK FOR

### Indigo for the colour table

Indigo is dark blue, blue to which black has been added. It is a strong, quiet, useful colour. A policeman's uniform is dark blue. Indigo is the background colour of the British flag. It is the colour of the night sky, and of ink. You might find some dark blue pansies at this time of year. If you stand a rose in ink, the edges of the petals will turn blue.

### Differences

As well as your colour table, try other sorting schemes. Have a table for dolls from different countries to show different kinds of people and costumes. Have an animal collection to show how animals are different from one another, different as a group from humans, and from things that don't live and breathe. Insects and plants are two other groups. Can the children discover what each set of things has in common? Make puzzles with three objects from one set of things and one from another. Can the children tell which object doesn't belong? Think together of all the things that come in pairs, like shoes, gloves, twins, wings; then knife and fork, girl and boy, pepper and salt, right and left.

### Symmetry

Look for the symmetry in sets of things. See how useful symmetry is. Our bodies are symmetrical. Arms and legs balance on each side. Look at a cow. The only thing it seems to have one of is a tail—and that is set right in the middle of its back, where it can flick each side of its body equally to keep off flies.

## TO JOIN IN

### Movement

Can anybody bring a mechanical doll to look at—a wind-up clockwork walking doll or a dancing doll on a music box? Then have the children try to imitate the actions of a mechanical toy. They can be stiff dollies, toy soldiers, daleks and robots. Pretend to wind them up again when they come to a standstill.

Play 'musical statues'. The children move around freely, exploring all the space and different ways of moving, while the music plays. When it stops, they must 'freeze' as they are until the music starts again.

### Stories

These three stories fit in with this week's themes. However, they are rather long for this age group. You could select particularly appealing adventures within the stories, and tell them to the children in your own words.

PINOCCHIO, by Carlo Collodi
TOM THUMB, by Grimm
THUMBELINA, by Hans Christian Andersen

### Action rhyme

Two fat gentlemen met in a lane, (Thumbs)
Bowed most politely, bowed once again.
Said, 'How do you do' and 'How do you do',
And 'How do you do' again.

Two thin ladies, etc. (Index fingers)
Two tall policemen, etc. (Middle fingers)
Two little schoolboys, etc. (Fourth fingers)
Two little babies, etc. (Little fingers)

All join hands and walk in a circle to:

A-ring, a-ring o' roses,
A pocket full of posies,
A-tishoo! A-tishoo!
We all fall down.

## TO INVESTIGATE

### Thumb puppets

Make Thumbelina and Tom Thumb puppets for children by drawing a face on your two thumbnails and wrapping a handkerchief around each for clothes.

You can also turn one thumb into a baby. Draw a face on the nail. Wrap a handkerchief over its head and around it as a shawl. Cup the other hand to make a cradle and put the thumb puppet into it. Help the children to wrap up their thumbs, using sticky tape where necessary.

### Finger puppets

The children draw around 10p pieces on paper, and cut out the circles. An adult will have to cut a curved slit in each circle for the finger to go through. Draw a face (the slit is where the chin would be). Remind the children about the sets of two eyes, two lips, two ears, one nose in the centre. Place faces on fingertips, facing in towards palm of hand. Your finger puppets could begin their show with the action rhyme, then develop original voices and characters.

You can make a finger puppet theatre by pushing the drawer out of a small matchbox, and putting two fingers through the drawer sleeve. The finger puppets could become Punch and Judy.

### Hand puppets

Draw Humpty Dumpty on the back of your hand, using two fingers as his legs. Open two matchboxes a little and close them tightly on your index and middle

fingers for shoes. Fold other fingers behind. Make Humpty do a tap dance. Let the other hand join in. Act out 'Jack and Jill went up the Hill' with two hands. Let the children try.

Make a hand puppet with a moving mouth by clenching your fist, thumb tucked in. With a felt pen, paint lips around thumb and index finger space. Draw eyes above on index finger knuckle. Now move your thumb up and down to make the mouth talk or bite somebody's finger.

Draw a face on the palm of your hand. Move your hand in different ways to make the expression change.

## TO CREATE

### Jig-jog puppets

This requires adult preparation. Draw or trace a human figure (unisex boy/girl or clown) and an animal shape, such as a dog, inside the back of a breakfast cereal packet. Cut out the body and head as one piece. Cut out the limbs and tail separately, allowing for overlap with the body.

Using packets as a source of cardboard, first glue a different, plain-coloured piece of paper on the back of each pack. Then arrange your pattern pieces, remembering to have half the human limbs facing right, and the other half left. All the animal limbs face in the same direction.

With an awl, pierce holes where limbs, tails and bodies are to be joined. Cut out. Mix all the bodies and limbs together. The children have to sort out which sets of limbs go with which bodies. When they have arranged left and right arms and legs for humans, pin the figure loosely together with brass paper fasteners. Animals should have four legs, two on each side. Fasten loosely. The children can hold the puppets in their hands and sway them to music or dangle them from a piece of string. The puppets can also be fastened to rods with sticky tape, and waved to make them move.

### An arm puppet

Details under 'Things for adults to make'

### Look at

NAMES, SETS AND NUMBERS, by Jeanne Bendick (Franklin Watts)

## TO TALK ABOUT

### Silkworms

June is the month for silkworms. Can anybody bring some to playgroup for everyone to see at the various stages of development? Outdoors, look about for mulberry trees. Their broad, light green leaves are very distinctive. Mulberry leaves are the main diet of silkworms. In a hot climate mulberry trees produce luscious indigo-red berries. In Britain they are usually planted in parks or along pavements for their shady green leaves.

About forty days after a silkworm hatches from a tiny egg, it begins to spin a cocoon of silk, from which it emerges as an egg-laying moth. The silken thread around the cocoon can be unwound and woven into silk material. Does any adult have a silk scarf that the children can look at and feel? Show how you can crumple it up small because the thread is so fine. Let go, and see how it springs back to its original size.

## TO LOOK FOR

### Fruit in the shops now

Apricots, cherries, currants, gooseberries, peaches, plums, strawberries

## TO JOIN IN

### Nursery rhyme

*A needle and thread*

Old Mother Twitchett had but one eye,
And a long tail, which she let fly;
And every time she went through a gap,
A bit of her tail she left in the trap.

### Action rhymes

'1, 2, 3, 4, 5—once I caught a fish alive.' (see April week 3)

10 little soldiers standing in a row. (fingers and thumbs)
They bowed to the captain, so!
They marched to the left. They marched to the right.
Then they marched straight home to sleep all night!

Little Jack Horner sat in a corner,
Eating his Christmas pie.
He put in his thumb and pulled out a plum.
And said, what a good boy am I.

Make a game with the children in which they have to shout out whether you put in your left or your right thumb each time you act this out. Can they show you which is their own left and right thumb? Understanding which is the left and which is the right becomes important as the children begin to learn kerb drill.

'Look right, look left, look right again—listen—give any cars that are coming time to pass; look right, look left, look right—and listen again. When all is clear, quick march!'

If children have joined the ROSPA Tufty road safety club and received badges, it is suggested that the badge be worn on the right-hand-side to help the child remember which way to look first. If you are doing this you must make sure that the badge is always on the right so that the child is not confused. Try to think of some other way of working out which is the right, like putting chalk on the right shoe, or a felt pen 'kiss' on the right hand, so that there is a double check. Under-fives are much too young to cross the road without an adult. Be alert to exceptions to the 'look right first' rule, like one-way streets and holidays abroad.

## TO INVESTIGATE

### Preserving summer

Help the children to gather full-blown rose petals, and steep them in jars of water to make rose-water perfume.

From a bouquet of summer flowers, choose the brightest hued petals and leaves. Let the children rub them on white paper to see the natural dyes.

Press whole flowers between sheets of blotting paper or newspapers, under a heavy book. In three days' time, when the petals have quite dried out, sticky-tape them on a wall chart for identification. Make a wall chart with ears of wheat, barley and other grasses and common wildflowers.

There is a 'pot pourri' mix on the market that you might find useful. The children can gather flower heads and petals. Mix together in a bowl. Leave to dry in an airing cupboard for a fortnight. Stir in the pot pourri herbs and spices mixture. Store in bottles with the tops on for another two weeks. When the top is removed you have a pretty and sweet-smelling reminder of the summer to keep clothes and rooms fragrant all winter.

## TO CREATE

### A petal-gathering bag

For each bag you will need a rectangle of strong brown paper 20 × 40 cm (8″ × 16″). Help the children to fold the paper in half. Show them how to seal two sides with gummed brown paper sealing tape, leaving one side open. A damp sponge can be used for wetting the gum. Stick two lengths of sealing tape together and attach as a shoulder strap.

The same sort of bag can be made out of torn-up old sheets, roughly sewn. A tie-and-dye session can transform them into works of art. Using the same principle, the children can also make small bags to fill with dried lavender or pot pourri. Sew up the last side after filling.

Find some rectangles of tough plastic—an old plastic tablecloth cut up would do—and a hole punch. Fold the rectangles in half and punch holes along the sides so that the children just have to thread through the holes. This is a good introduction to the in-and-out movement of sewing. You can make the end of the yarn stiff for threading with sticky tape, dried glue or sealing wax.

### Window box

This can be used as a holder for letters waiting to be answered. It would make a pretty and useful gift for Father's Day.

1  Select a small size cereal packet. Glue the top opening flap firmly in place. Cut it in half across the width. Each half makes a separate window box.
2  Cut away a section of the front, leaving a frame on two sides and at the bottom.
3  The children can paint the outside of the boxes in a strong colour to cover the print. (Powder paint including some white, mixed with neat detergent, will cover most print.) The inside is best painted sky blue.

4  When the paint is dry, the children can sticky-tape pressed flowers and leaves inside the back of the box. If you use the widest sticky tape obtainable, it will protect most of the flowers.

Of course, the children can stick grass and flowers in any packet with the front and one long side removed, at any time, just for fun.

## TO FOLLOW UP

### Cloth weaving

Can anybody bring a small hand weaving loom to show how cloth is made? Some of the children could experiment with weaving coloured yarn in and out of squares cut from old string vests, or open-weave dish cloths.

### Paper weaving

Take a 20 cm (7½″) square of strong paper. Rule it into 2 cm (¾″) strips, leaving a 2 cm (¾″) frame all around. With a blade or scalpel, cut a slit between each strip, leaving the frame intact. Now rule and cut eight loose 20 × 2 cm (7½″ × ¾″) strips in a contrasting colour.

A woven pattern is created when a child threads the loose strips under and over the framed strips in alternate rows.

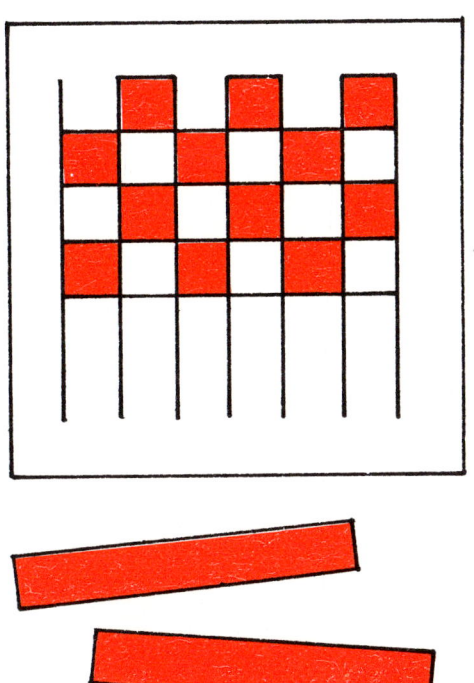

### Look at

ABOUT SILKWORMS AND SILK, Junior Look, Read, and Learn Series 1 (Muller)

## TO TALK ABOUT

### High summer

June 21 is the longest day of the year, when the sun is directly overhead; and the shortest night. June 24 is midsummer's day. Many people believe the fairies dance from midnight until dawn on midsummer's night. In some countries people light fires on midsummer's night to encourage the sun to shine warmly all summer. There definitely seems to be a magical excitement in the air that makes people feel like celebrating. Show the children pictures of the ancient stone circle at Stonehenge, where the druids still celebrate midsummer in England.

Country lore says that midsummer may be our last opportunity to hear the cuckoo and nightingale this year.

## TO LOOK FOR

### Plant life

June is a leafy month, with roses in full bloom, honeysuckle in hedges, bees visiting the foxgloves (which are poisonous plants). The wild rose blooms from now until August. Bracken fronds unfurl. Look for yellow ragwort, ragged robin, goosegrass with its tiny hooks and greenish-white flowers, carnations, honesty, pansies, snapdragons. The farmers begin hay-making while the sun shines.

## TO JOIN IN

### Movement

Enjoy a good old pagan dance around some central point, like a circle of stones used as an imaginary fire. Besides free expression, include characteristic dance movements that the children may have seen on film of American Indians, African Bushmen, Australian Aborigines, Maoris, ancient Egyptians.

### Record

'Sun A-rise', by Rolf Harris on MFP 7″ record.

### Shadow play

Make a game of jumping on your own shadow. The children will soon find that it can't be done, but they will enjoy trying. Next they could try jumping on someone else's shadow. Can they make their shadows dance? Can they make two shadows shake hands without physically touching one another? Can they make a shadow of one body with many arms by standing one behind the other? If they stand in a spaced line one behind the other, with arms outstretched, their shadows can do a circus trick, balancing on each other's heads. What other tricks can shadows play? What shapes can the children make with hand shadows?

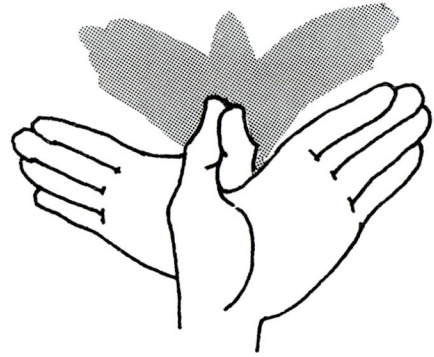

### Rhymes

*Mr Nobody*

As I was walking up the stair
I met a man who wasn't there.
He wasn't there again today.
I wish, I wish, he'd stay away!
(Could Mr Nobody be a shadow?)

Now I am tall, (stretch up)
Now I am small. (crouch down)
Funny shadow on the wall!

'My Shadow', from A CHILD'S GARDEN OF VERSE, by R. L. Stevenson.

## TO INVESTIGATE

### Shadow uses

Strong sunlight casts strong shadows, which is just as well because animals, insects and people need to rest in the shade on very hot days.

We can tell the time of day by the length of the shadows. Explain to the children that as the sun rises in the morning over the eastern horizon, it throws long shadows to the west. The shadows grow shorter as the sun rises in the sky. When the sun is directly above us at midday, there is hardly any shadow at all. The shadows gradually lengthen to the east as the sun sinks in the west and night falls.

You can demonstrate this. Early in the morning ask a child to stand in the garden. Draw around his feet or mark the place with pebbles. Draw or mark out the outline of the child's shadow. Repeat this at midday and mid-afternoon. How has the shadow changed?

Is there a sundial in your district? Perhaps you could take the children to see how the sun tells the time. Build your own 'Stonehenge' outdoors with a circle of rocks, and note how the shadows change during the day. The real Stonehenge is thought to be a clock of the year.

## TO CREATE

### Handkerchief sun hats

Hat No 1   Take a large handkerchief. Tie a knot in each corner to give it a rounded shape.

Hat No 2   Fold a large handkerchief in half, then in half again. Lift it so that you have three thicknesses of fabric on one side, and one thickness on the other, and place it on the head.

The children could copy as you demonstrate, using squares torn from old sheets.

### Newspaper sun hats

See 'Things for adults to make'

### A parachute man

Tie equal lengths of cotton thread to each corner of a handkerchief. Tie a plastic toy man to the thread. Fold handkerchief in your hand. Throw in the air and watch the parachute open.

### A sun chart

Warn the children not to look directly at the sun!

Look for the sun early in the morning through a window. Make a cross with masking tape on the window where the sun appears. Check the sun's position at regular intervals during the day, and mark it with a cross. Make notes of the times and stick them on the window. Look to see if the sun repeats this pattern every day.

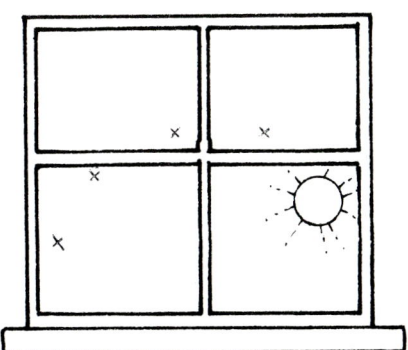

## TO FOLLOW UP

### Silhouettes

Do the children know what a profile is? It is the side view of the face, with the nose sticking out. We don't normally see our own profile because it is so difficult to look sideways in the mirror.

Do the children know what a silhouette is? It is a dark shape against a light background. A shadow is one kind of silhouette.

You could paint a silhouette of each child's profile. Stand a child between an easel and the sun, so that the shadow of his profile is cast on your drawing paper. With black paint, draw around the outline of his shadow. Now fill it in with black.

The children might like to try painting your silhouette now. Paint silhouettes of a teddy and a doll shape.

# JUNE

## TO TALK ABOUT

### Phases of the moon

On warm evenings watch for the waxing and waning of the moon. It takes a month (one moonth) for the moon to change from new crescent to full circle and back again. Sometimes the moon can tell us about coming weather conditions. For instance, 'A ring around the moon means rain soon.' Have any of the children noticed a ring of haze around the moon at some time? This is called a 'watery moon'.

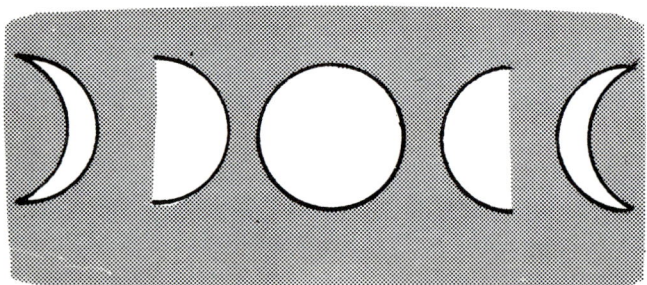

Do the children know the name for that extra daylight period we enjoy in summer, which makes it so hard to go to bed early? It is a pretty name—twilight! The sun disappears at dusk and reappears at dawn. Can the children tell you any little stories about twilight, dusk and dawn?

Print any prose poems they might unconsciously create. See if they can paint a picture of what they were thinking, and display the two together. You might feel that the results are worth making into a book about the sky for the whole group to enjoy.

## TO LOOK FOR

### Wildlife

Yellowhammer bird. In the country, look for little mounds of earth that tell you a mole has burrowed underneath. The baby moles are about six weeks old now.

### Weather

Can be very warm. Check thermometer. Has temperature reached 21°C?

## TO JOIN IN

### Action song

All join hands and skip around the ring, first one way and then the other, singing:

Sally go round the sun, (change)
Sally go round the moon. (change)
Sally go round the chimney pots,
On a Saturday afternoon.

### Games with a skipping rope

Let the children take turns at jumping the rope held at different levels. You can vary the height to suit the age and ability of each child.

Lay the rope flat on the ground and send 'waves' along it. See if the children can jump the waves. Vary the height according to each child's ability.

Turn the rope in the usual manner, making large, gentle sweeps. The children take turns at running through under the rope. Once again, a sensitive hand on the rope helps the tinies through.

Skipping chant:

Draw a pail of water,
For my lady's daughter.
One rush, two rush,
Prithee, fine lady,
Jump over the bush.

For running under the rope:

Prithee, fine lady (or laddie),
Run under my bush.

### Nursery rhymes

The man in the moon came tumbling down,
And asked the way to Norwich;
He went by the south, and burnt his mouth
With eating cold pease porridge.

The man in the moon looked out of the moon,
Looked out of the moon and said,
'Tis time for all children on the earth
To think about going to bed!'

'Wynken, Blynken and Nod' (BOOK OF A THOUSAND POEMS)

'Hey, diddle diddle', 'There was an old woman toss'd up in a basket' (PUFFIN BOOK OF NURSERY RHYMES)

**Story**

'Many Moons', by James Thurber from A BOOK OF PRINCESSES (Penguin)

## TO INVESTIGATE

### Shapes

Many things in nature are round in shape. The earth is round. The sun is round. The moon is round. Some seeds are round. We turn around. What else can the children think of that is round?

Round things don't stack very well. To stack or build we need flat surfaces. Blocks and bricks are square and rectangular. What else can the children think of that has an angular shape?

Fold gummed paper squares and cut along the folds to produce smaller squares, rectangles, triangles, hexagons and pentagons. Cut out some circles and irregular shapes too. Let the children make up their own patterns and pictures, sticking them down when they are satisfied with them. Discuss any discoveries about the way shapes fit together, overlap, change, look flat or solid, remind us of things.

Save breakfast cereal packets. Cut a basic shape out of the front of each to make a frame. Save interesting full page pictures from magazines. Paste them on cardboard. The children can insert them in the cereal packet frames to investigate the different masking effects.

Set out toy building bricks so that the children can quietly reinforce their understanding of how flat surfaces stack.

## TO CREATE

### Clay play

The children can begin by making a round shape. That could be the moon. Next they can make some of the creatures that come out at night, nocturnal creatures. A round shape with a snout might be a mole. Stick in half matchsticks and it could be a hedgehog. A round body, snout, ears and tail make a mouse. A small circle on top of a larger one can become a cat or an owl. Round shapes squashed could be stones. Add a thick stem and they are mushrooms. (You could mention that some real mushrooms and toadstools are poisonous. They are best left where they grow unless an adult is supervising.)

If you can spare an old tray or piece of board on which models could be arranged, some sort of night scene might suggest itself to the children.

Let the children feel the changed texture of clay when it has dried into a shape. Leave clay models to dry out for at least a week. Then paint with shellac to keep moisture out so that models stay in good condition.

For the children, investigating what clay is and what can be done with it is more important than producing a recognisable shape.

## TO FOLLOW UP

### A contour map

Take advantage of June sunshine to let the children play out of doors with papier mâché on a large board. You could mix in a bag of sawdust from a pet shop. Flowers can be stuck in it to make a garden, or roadways can be levelled, mountains moulded, and rivers channelled. City children may never have seen real mountains and valleys, so discuss these with them. When the papier mâché has hardened into a contour map, toy soldiers can march across it, cowboys and Indians can hide in it, cars can drive through it, or farm animals can graze on it.

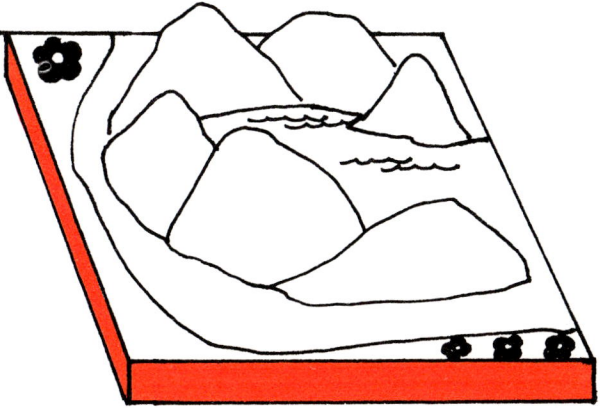

### Papier mâché recipe

1  Make up wallpaper paste in a bucket, about one-third full.
2  Tear newspapers up into small pieces. Put them in the bucket.
3  Stir well. Allow to soak for a while. Squeeze out and model with it.

### We are here

With the children contributing information, draw a simple map of the roads leading to your play centre. Make a note of where each child joins the main route.

# JULY

# week 1

## TO TALK ABOUT

### Making copies

Have you got a photograph of yourself that you can show to the children? Do the children have any photographs of themselves that they would like to bring to playgroup? You could have a portrait gallery!

A photograph is a copy of one's likeness. A reflection in a mirror is another kind of copy, and a shadow is another.

There is something in nature that has a copy of itself, just like looking in a mirror. It is a bivalve shell. Do you have some that the children can look at? There are many kinds of bivalves, from the giant clam to the delicate butterfly shell we find washed up on the beach, empty but still joined.

Two things the same joined together make useful tools. Look at a pair of scissors, a nut cracker, pliers, vice, spring clothes pegs, door handles.

This week, see what you can discover about copies.

## TO LOOK FOR

### Violet for the colour table

Violet is the final colour in the rainbow. It is made up of blue and red. Many flowers that bloom in July are violet, mauve and purple in colour. A violet is violet. All the flowers from a violet plant are copies of each other. They even smell the same.

Some butterflies have splashes of violet colouring. If you are very lucky you might see a Purple Emperor. Purple is a very rich colour, deeper than violet. It is often used for royal robes. Have you any scraps of purple velvet for the colour table?

## TO JOIN IN

### Movement

*A butterfly dance*

The children dart about fluttering paper wings, streamers, or scarves.

*A butterfly kiss*

Flutter your eyelashes against the cheek of a child.

Do the children wonder why butterflies are called butterflies? Flutterbys seems a much better name!

## Poems

*In the mirror*

In the mirror
On the wall,
There's a face
I always see;
Round and pink,
And rather small,
Looking back again
At me.

It is very
Rude to stare,
But she never
Thinks of that,
For her eyes are
Always there;
What can she be
Looking at?

Elizabeth Fleming

*The Butterfly*

I know a little butterfly
With tiny golden wings,
He plays among the summer flowers
And up and down he swings,
He dances on their honey cups
So happy all the day,
And then he spreads his tiny wings—
And softly flies away.

Margaret Rose

## TO INVESTIGATE

### Office science

Provide each child with two sheets of paper with a sheet of carbon paper in between. Show them how to hold a pencil and take a line for a walk, in readiness for writing.

Take out the carbon and look at the magical reproduction.

Can anybody supply outdated office rubber stamps and a stamp pad? Decorate a grocery carton to look like a post box for posting playgroup letters.

## Splodge art

1  Show the children how to fold a piece of paper down the centre.
2  Open it out.
3  Make a paint or ink splodge to one side of centre.
4  Fold the paper over again and smooth firmly.
5  Open out and see what your splodge looks like doubled. It may remind you of a butterfly, a crab, a carrot. . . . Draw around it if an outline helps to make the likeness stronger.

## Finger painting

Mix some powder paint good and thick with wallpaper paste. Dollop it onto a tray, removable washing machine top, or a vinyl table top. Roll the children's sleeves up or cover them with plastic pull-ons. Now the children can put their hands into the paint and make all kinds of patterns. You can take a print off the patterns they like best by pressing on and smoothing a clean sheet of paper. The children will find it very natural to use two hands together, making identical patterns. A butterfly is a common result.

## TO CREATE

### A clip-on butterfly

When the children's finger-paint butterflies have dried, they could be cut out and glued to a spring clothes peg. Clip butterflies all around your room.

### A butterfly mobile

Fold spare butterflies double, bending the wings out at right-angles. Glue the folded body together, inserting a length of black cotton thread. Hang them from a coat hanger or a length of thread stretched high across the room. Aeroplanes can be made like this too.

## Dressing-up wings (1–4 preparation for the adult to demonstrate)

1  Fold a large sheet of brown paper in half.
2  Measure the length of a child's arm. Draw a wing shape to fit, away from the fold.
3  Cut out through both sheets of paper.
4  Make two half-loops of gummed brown paper strips along the underside of each wing for the child's arms to slot through.
5  The child can paint the wings.
6  Peg them out to dry just as a newly hatched insect has to hold his wings out to dry in the sun before he can fly away.

## Feathery wings (for the children to copy)

1  Take two sheets of newspaper. Fold at centre fold 'gutter'.
2  Dealing with one double sheet at a time, cut thin strips from bottom edge to within 5 cm (2″) of the centre fold.
3  Place one sheet over each of the child's arms. Tie in place with string.

## TO FOLLOW UP

### The mirror game

Two children face each other. One is the leader and the other is the mirror. Everything the leader does, the mirror has to copy. Then they change over.

## TO TALK ABOUT

### A teddy bears' picnic

July 15 is St Swithin's day. A superstition says that if it rains on St Swithin's day, it will rain for forty days. In fact, the last two weeks of July can be very wet indeed, so it would be a good idea to take advantage of the sunshine while it lasts to have a teddy bears' picnic outdoors. There is a great variety of delicious fruit in the shops now. Perhaps everybody could bring a piece of fruit to eat at the picnic.

Talk over with the children all the things you could do, so that they can join in the fun of planning the picnic. You could bake cakes to take. An adult might bring a camera to take pictures. Discuss your route so that the children know exactly what to expect and what is expected of them. Enlist as much adult help with supervision as possible. Invite everybody's teddy or favourite doll. Request that teddies and dolls wear a name tag to avoid mix-ups. Act out in advance some of the things that you might do at the picnic.

### String along

You might find it helpful to take a long piece of string or a skipping rope, which each child can hold onto with one hand on alternate sides as you make your way to the picnic spot. This is fun to do, gives a feeling of security, keeps the pace steady, and identifies you as a group so that you are not split up by other pedestrians.

## TO LOOK FOR

### Fruit in the shops now

Apricots, cantaloup melon, watermelon, cherries, currants, gooseberries, loganberries, peaches, plums, raspberries, rhubarb, strawberries, furry-shelled beech nuts

## TO JOIN IN

Before or after your visit to the picnic spot, play the record, 'A Teddy Bears' Picnic' (CHILDREN'S FAVOURITES, MFP 1175). Some of the children might like to do free expression dancing, some could clap the rhythm, others could join in with musical instruments. It could also be used as background music to listen to for inspiration while painting.

### Poem

'Lines and Squares', from WHEN WE WERE VERY YOUNG, by A. A. Milne

### Song

'The bear went over the mountain' see April, week 2. Add last verse,

Oh, we won't be home 'till morning,
We won't be home 'till morning,
We won't be home 'till morning,
(SHOUT) And maybe not at all!

### Action game

Adults often say things that seem very strange to little children, for instance, 'Sit here for the present'. 'What present?'

'Are you the only one in your family?' 'No, I have a mother and a father. Did you think I lived by myself?'

There will always be funny misunderstandings, but we can help to make the meaning of some words clear by acting them out in a game.

'Where's the bear?' teaches place words. Ask another adult to help the children the first couple of times you play it.

Leader: Oh, look! *There's* a bear!
Children: *Where's* a bear?
Leader: *Under* your chair!
Children (after looking): There's no bear there!
Leader (pointing): *Up* in the air!
Children: There's no bear there!
Leader: *Through* the window!
Children: There's no bear there!
Leader: *Outside* the door!
Children: There's no bear there!
Leader: *Beside* Judy!
Children: There's no bear there!
Leader: *Behind* Mark!
Children: There's no bear there!
Leader (While the children are still looking behind):
    It's *in front* of you now!

Children: There's no bear there!
Leader: It's . . . *around* the corner!
Children: There's no bear there!
Leader: *On top* of the cupboard!
Children: There's no bear there!
Leader (looks in cupboard): *In* the cupboard!
Children: There's the bear!
Leader (turning around): Where?
Children: Behind you!
Leader: There's no bear there!
Children: In front of you!
Leader: There's no bear there!

The children will shout out a lot of different suggestions at once. Try to follow up each one, repeating the place word as you look for the bear. You could end up back at the cupboard. Look in, find it empty.

Leader: That's not fair!
Children shout: We don't care!

If you are playing this game outdoors, hunt *behind* trees, *under* hedges, *in* a bush, etc.

## Stories

Your own favourite from the *Pooh Bear* books, by A. A. Milne

THE FORGOTTEN BEAR, by Molly Brett (The Medici Society)

GOLDILOCKS AND THE THREE BEARS, version by Paul Galdone (World's Work)

LITTLE BEAR, by Else Homelund Minarik (World's Work)

## TO INVESTIGATE

### Playing with pastry

The children could make some real cakes to take on their picnic. Make them a day in advance. If you are dealing with a couple of 6–7 year olds, weighing and measuring ingredients and blending them correctly is well worth doing. You could make gingerbread or shortbread. But if you are dealing with 20 under-fives, the quick results and simple steps of a packet of short pastry mix more than make up for the lack of flavour. The children can rehearse the whole process first with playdough.

*Non-edible pastry for play*

(It won't do any harm if some of this is eaten, but it won't taste very nice.)

Ingredients:

1 cup of flour
1 tablespoon of salt
Water

Method:

Mix flour and salt in a large bowl. Add enough water to make a stiff, non-sticky dough. Knead it. Add more flour if necessary. Add vegetable dye if you like. This dough will keep for a week if wrapped in polythene after each playing session. The children can roll it out with rolling pins, and cut it into shapes and 'gingerbread men' with pastry cutters.

*Edible short pastry biscuits and baked bears*

Ingredients:

1 packet of short pastry mix
1 tablespoon of sugar
Water

Method:

Mix pastry and sugar in a large bowl. Add enough water to make a stiff, non-sticky dough. Knead it. Roll it out on a floured board. Cut it into shapes and 'gingerbread men' with pastry cutters. Wet a little bit of pastry to make it stick, and add ears to the gingerbread men to turn them into bears. Use currants for eyes and nose, and a slice of glazed cherry for a mouth.

If you have an oven at playgroup, place the biscuits on a greased baking tray and put in a moderate oven. Do not let the children near the hot stove. Do not over-cook the biscuits. They won't take long. Cool and store for the picnic. If you haven't an oven on the premises, arrange for an adult to take them home to bake.

## TO CREATE

The children might like to paint their impression of the picnic afterwards.

### A teddy do-up doll

See 'Things for adults to make'

## TO FOLLOW UP

### Take a camera

This is your chance to get some delightful studies of the children unselfconsciously enjoying themselves, in ideal (let's hope) light conditions. Even the shyest child is likely to hold her teddy up to have his photo taken. It is a good idea to take black-and-white as well as colour film, as it makes a less expensive record for the playgroup pin-board. These pictures will give fresh delight in years to come when those toddlers are grown-up school children. Parents will probably not mind a small profit being made towards playgroup funds on prints they order.

## TO TALK ABOUT

### Flower power

'Fairy clocks' are easy to find growing in July. The children can blow away the hours of the day on them. They are really a cluster of dandelion seedlings waiting for the wind to carry them off to fertile ground. Can the children see how well-designed they are for flying? If you want to bring one into play-group to talk about, spray it with hair lacquer before you pick it and it will stay intact.

When the children are playing daisy chains, begin a search for a lucky four-leafed clover. As clover leaves are divided into three, the children will be very lucky indeed if they find a four-leafed one.

The children may see poppies popping up in country fields. If you turn one inside out and tie a blade of grass around the petals for a waist, it looks like a lady in a long red dress.

Sweet peas are flowers that have 'hands'. The tendrils help the plant to climb up wire screens. Let the children feel the power of those clinging springs.

Shell some eating peas. Make the pods go 'pop'. Taste how sweet the smallest peas are. If you start off with half a kilogramme (one pound) of peas in shells, weigh the peas when they have been shelled. Add the shells to bring the weight back to half a kilogramme (one pound) again. Turn the pods into boats with paper sail and matchstick mast fixed in plasticine.

## TO LOOK FOR

### Plant life

Wild, blue forget-me-nots along river banks, field scabious, Scarlet Pimpernel, a tiny red flower whose petals close when rain threatens; hemlock, deadly nightshade (both poisonous), hydrangea, red hot poker, sweet pea, clematis, Sweet William, lavender and coleus, with its many-coloured leaves. Warn children never to eat any kind of berries without checking with an adult first.

## TO JOIN IN

### Ball games

Play some of these ball games out of doors.

1 All the children sit in a ring and roll a ball from one to the other.

2 Stand in the centre of a circle and see if the children can catch a gentle throw. If not, roll the ball to each child in turn, who then rolls it back to you.

3 Let the children experiment with rolling the ball between their legs, as in tunnel ball, individually, then joining together to make a long tunnel.

### Action rhyme

Five portly peas in a pea-pod pressed, (fingers of one hand curled under)
One grew, two grew, and so did all the rest. (fingers and thumb gradually uncurl)
They grew and they grew and they didn't stop, (stretch fingers)
Until one day the pod went 'pop'! (clap hands)

### Nursery rhymes

Lavender's blue, dilly dilly,
Lavender's green.
If I were king, dilly dilly,
You would be queen.

Call out your men, dilly dilly,
Set them to work,
Some to make hay, dilly dilly,
Some to cut corn.
Some to make hay, dilly dilly,
Some to cut corn,
Whilst you and I, dilly dilly,
Keep ourselves warm.

Mary, Mary, quite contrary,
How does your garden grow?
With silver bells and cockle shells,
And pretty maids all in a row.

(Music for these rhymes is in THE OXFORD NURSERY SONG BOOK)

### Poem

'O dandelion, yellow as gold,
What do you do all day?'
'I just wait here in the tall green grass
'Till the children come to play.'
'O dandelion, yellow as gold,

What do you do all night?'
'I wait and wait 'till the cool dew falls
And my hair grows long and white.'
'And what do you do when your hair is white
And the children come to play?'
'They take me up in their dimpled hands
And blow my hair away!'

## TO INVESTIGATE

### Veins

Look at the leaves on a flower stem with the children. They have veins. Look at the wings of a butterfly. They have veins. Examine the children's hands. They have veins. Show them your hands. The veins are probably a little more pronounced than those of the children. Ask the children to look at a grandma's hands, and notice if they can see the veins plainly. The children might like to know that the blood in our veins carries the goodness from the food we eat round our bodies, right to the very tips of our fingers and toes. Do the children know the names for all the parts of the hand—knuckles, joints, nails, palm, back, wrist? Continue up to your elbow, shoulder, and shoulder blade. Legs have funny names too—ankle, shin, knee!

The children could make prints of the veins in a leaf. It is easiest if they sticky-tape a leaf to a piece of paper first, at the tip and stem, veined side facing out. They can press the veined side on a stamp pad or piece of foam sponge dipped in paint. Then press the leaf into another piece of paper, smoothing it down firmly with the hand over the backing paper. Draw a tall tree trunk for each child to print leaves all around, or let one leaf print equal one tree in a landscape, or let the children make a higgledy-piggledy pattern of leaf prints. You could do one like this yourself and finish it off with a bird face and legs, or make it into some other fanciful creature. The children might see imaginary animals in their own patterns. You could make a chart with prints of different kinds of leaves, naming the type of plant they came from.

## TO CREATE

### Stained glass windows

Stained glass windows have veins of black leading to hold the small pieces in place. The children could make their own stained glass windows, using squares cut from the waxed paper inside breakfast cereal packets. Have the children seated at a table. Place a square, waxed side up, in front of each child. Place a box of odds and ends of paper in the centre of the table, including things like little mermaids cut from bath cube wrappers, sweet papers, light coloured cloth snippets, scraps of tissue paper. The children can create a design on the waxed paper. Make sure that there is a little space between all the pieces, for the wax to form a seal. Then place another square, wax side down on top of the first piece. Press with a hot iron. The wax will melt, sealing the pieces in place. You could bind the edges with black passé partout. Sticky-tape the squares to a window to see the light shine through. Talk about things that are transparent and things that are opaque.

Another way to make stained glass windows is for the children to fold a sheet of black paper and cut holes along the folded edges as if making a paper doily. Unfold, press flat, and stick a sheet of coloured cellophane or tissue paper across the back so that it shows through the holes.

## TO FOLLOW UP

### Lavender bags

Now is the time to pick lavender. Dry the flowers between sheets of blotting paper or newspapers, under a heavy book, for at least three days.

To make the bag, trace circles onto muslin using a saucer. The children will need good pinking shears to cut the material. Using darning needles with thread tied on, and a large knot, the children could sew around the edge of the circle. Place lavender in the centre, draw the thread in and tie it tightly for the children.

Horse Chestnut
palmate shape

Rose leaf
serrated edge

Holly
dentate edge

Privet
entire edge

Ground Ivy
crenate edge

# JULY                    week 4

## TO TALK ABOUT

### The dog days

July and August may be very hot, and have frequent thunderstorms. They are sometimes called the 'dog days' because this weather coincides with the rising of the dog star constellation in the night sky.

Some people are frightened of thunderstorms. If you are one of them, do your best not to convey your fear to the children. Treat this natural phenomenon naturally. Be sympathetic to any terror that the children may feel.

Pre-storm atmosphere often makes people feel tense. There is a build-up of electricity in the air until it is discharged as lightning and thunder. So you could tell the children that most people enjoy a good thunderstorm because it releases the pent-up energy and relieves our tension. A good downpour of rain washes everything clean and fresh, and helps the garden grow. You might even get a hailstorm in July. This is really exciting to watch from indoors, but it damages the garden flowers and farmers' crops. Warn the children that it is not a good idea to shelter under a tree if caught in a thunderstorm, because trees are prone to be struck by lightning. Look for a lightning conductor on top of a church steeple.

## TO LOOK FOR

### Wildlife

Dragonfly, peacock and red admiral butterflies, glow-worm, poisonous snakes, wasps. If on holiday at the seaside, look for cuttlefish and seagulls.

### Weather

Hot and stormy. What does the thermometer show this month?

## TO JOIN IN

### Movement

*'Danger' game*

Here's a game you may play to help use up the children's energy indoors, while it is raining outdoors.

The children pretend to be rabbits hopping and jumping about in a field. Happy music will help.

When you shout 'danger!', the music either stops or becomes menacing. The children must freeze exactly as they are for a count of five. Shout 'danger over!' and the rabbits begin to play again.

### Action rhyme

I hear thunder,
I hear thunder,
Oh, can't you?
Oh, can't you?
Pitter, patter raindrops,
Pitter, patter raindrops,
I'm wet through.
So are you!

### Nursery rhymes

Rain, rain, go away,
Come again another day,
Little Johnny wants to play.
(Personalise rhymes, using the names of children in your group, wherever practicable.)

It's raining, it's pouring,
The old man's snoring,
He went to bed and bumped his head,
And couldn't get up in the morning.

Rub-a-dub-dub,
Three men in a tub,
Who do you think they be?
The butcher, the baker, the candlestick maker,
Turn them out, knaves all three.

An adult can play this over and over again with three small children in a washing tub on the lawn, suiting the action to the words. For an only child, add two dolls.

*Washing day*

They that wash on Monday
Have all the week to dry;
They that wash on Tuesday
Are not so much awry;
They that wash on Wednesday
Are not so much to blame;
They that wash on Thursday

Wash for very shame;
They that wash on Friday
Wash in sorry need;
They that wash on Saturday
Are lazy folk indeed.

## TO INVESTIGATE

### Static electricity

When there's a lot of electricity in the air, the children may notice that their hair tends to stand on end when it is combed. They may see sparks fly from nylon underwear when they take it off at bedtime. Here are three experiments using static electricity.

1 Ask the children to tear some tissue paper into small pieces. Rub a plastic comb or ruler on your sleeve to create friction. Hold it close to the paper and it will attract the small pieces to itself. They will stick on and be quite hard to remove, jumping back on as you pull them off.

2 Similarly, if you rub a balloon on a woollen sweater, then hold it up to the wall, you will find it sticks to the wall.

3 Cut the top off a paper tissue box. Place pieces of coloured tissue paper in the bottom. Some could be cut out in the shape of ballerinas or fish. Place a sheet of clear plastic over the top, and attach with sticky tape. When the children rub the top, the pieces of paper will jump up and adhere to the plastic.

You might take this opportunity to explain to children that static electricity is nothing like as powerful as the electric current that runs through wires and is worked by switches in our homes. The lightning in the sky that is capable of blasting a tree is an example of its real power. Used correctly by adults to light rooms and work the iron and the vacuum cleaner, electricity is a great help to people. But it is *dangerous*. Plugs and switches must never be played with or experimented with..

## TO CREATE

### A balloon man

Bind round and long balloons together with sticky tape to make a giant or a Father Christmas. Stick on eyes, nose, and a cottonwool beard and eyebrows. A triangular cap can be made of red crêpe paper with cottonwool trim.

## TO FOLLOW UP

### Washing weather

While the children are home on holiday you have a good opportunity to wash playgroup linen, dressing-up clothes and dolls' clothes, and to air bedding. At some playgroups it is a tremendous help if mothers can organise a regular washing rota for tea towels, hand towels, etc., and for the very important job of lavatory cleaning.

Children on holiday at home could make the most of sunny weather to do their dolls' washing. Dolly pegs are not so easy to find these days, having been superseded by spring pegs, but they are still fun to dress, paint faces on, and for interlocking to make strange shapes. Hardware shops do have them occasionally. To make arms for a peg doll, place one pipe-cleaner through the legs. Turn ends up. Wind another pipe cleaner around the first to hold arms in place and to give a waist that will grip a skirt.

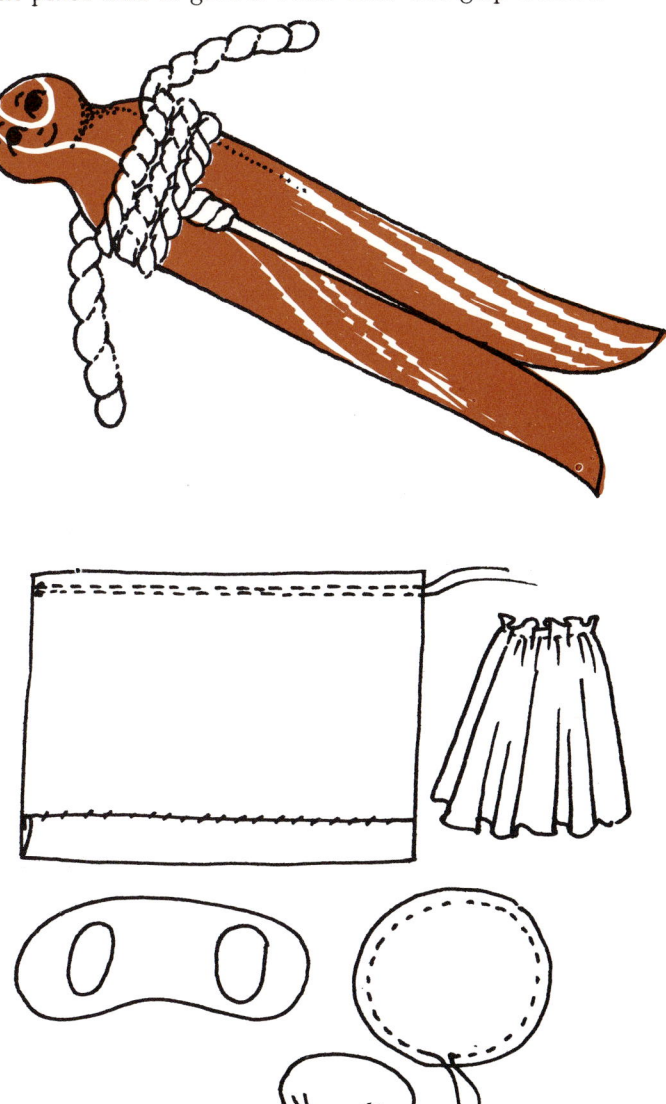

# AUGUST week 1

## TO TALK ABOUT

### What do pets eat?

Perhaps someone could bring a cage pet to playgroup for a morning? A real animal would make a good starting point for talking about what pets eat. Whether the pet is a bird, rabbit or rodent, it should be placed where it can be seen but not touched by unsupervised children. This is for mutual protection; children can frighten and torment pets, and open cage doors; pets can bite and scratch.

What a difference there is in the diet of pets! Even members of the same family, like rodents, eat vastly different things. Guinea pigs and mice eat vegetable and salad scraps. Gerbils eat grain and sunflower seeds. Do any of the children have pets? Talk about what their pets eat, if they live in a cage, if they go outdoors, etc.

## TO LOOK FOR

### Brown for the colour table

Brown is the colour of the good earth. Red, blue and yellow make brown. Most mixtures of three or more colours end up as brown. Some people have brown eyes. Some have brown hair. Some have brown skin. Count how many of each are in your group. Wooden furniture is often brown. Gerbils have golden brown fur.

Some of the most delicious things to eat are brown. Think of a crusty brown loaf of bread. Maybe you could try some. Think of chocolate and chocolate cake. Think of coconuts and cocoa. Think of brown soup and brown toast.

## TO JOIN IN

### Movement

All try nibbling at bread and nuts the way that pets do.

### Action songs

An owl flew down from an old oak tree,
(Put thumbs side by side, fingers outstretched like wings for owl.)
'Twiddle-a-whoo,' quoth he.

'Oh, little brown mouse,
Come out of your house,
I'd like you to come to tea, to tea,
I'd like you to come to tea.'

Out of a hole in the oak tree bowl,
(Make a hole with one hand. The index finger of other hand becomes the mouse peeping out.)
A little mouse looked to see,
Who asked her to come to tea, to tea,
Who asked her to come to tea.

'You're quite absurd,
You silly old bird,
To ask me to come to tea.
The tea you would eat is me, is me,
The tea you would eat is me!'

All sit and make hammering motion with one fist on knee, singing,

Peter hammers with one hammer, one hammer, one hammer,
Peter hammers with one hammer, and we all do the same.

Peter hammers with two hammers (two fists hammer)
Peter hammers with three hammers (tap with one foot as well)
Peter hammers with four hammers (tap with two feet, hammer with two fists)
Peter hammers with five hammers (nod with head also)

End with:

Peter is going to sleep now, sleep now, sleep now.
Peter is going to sleep now, and we all do the same.
(Music in THIS LITTLE PUFFIN)

### Record

Listen to PETER AND THE WOLF

## TO INVESTIGATE

### Growing grain

Sprinkle pet food grains on wet blotting paper to see what sprouts first. Keep it in a dark place until it germinates. Keep the blotting paper moist.

## Seed gathering time

Towards the end of summer many grasses, plants and trees grow seeds. Ask the children to help you collect many different kinds of seeds and grain. Use an example of each kind to make an identification chart. Glue some into montages, thread some for beads, and plant some to grow. Horse chestnuts grow fairly easily, but take a few months to germinate. Pierce horse chestnuts (conkers) with an awl to make them easy for the children to thread for beads. They might like to polish them with wax polish to preserve the shine.

## A taste and smell table

Set out a taste and smell table for brown things that are good to eat and drink. You could have a saucer of coffee and cocoa beans, cubes of toasted bread and brown bread, brown sugar, chocolate, gingerbread biscuits and anything else you can think of that would be interesting to taste or smell, and not harmful. This could be your most popular investigation ever. Print a large label for each item. Lower case letters and black ink on white card are best to give continuity when the children begin reading from books.

## TO CREATE

### Seed mosaics

1  Give each child a sheet of paper.
2  Using a spreader, each child covers the paper fairly evenly with glue.
3  Supply pet food seeds, seeds used in cooking (lentils, broad beans, split peas), and pasta shapes to make mosaic patterns. Set the seeds out on saucers down the centre of the table so that they are easy for all the children to reach. You might like to colour quantities of pasta with different vegetable dyes, and keep a box of each colour ready to use. Have an extra box for saving multicoloured odds and ends after each session. Gummed labels for your boxes, obtainable from stationers, are a useful investment.

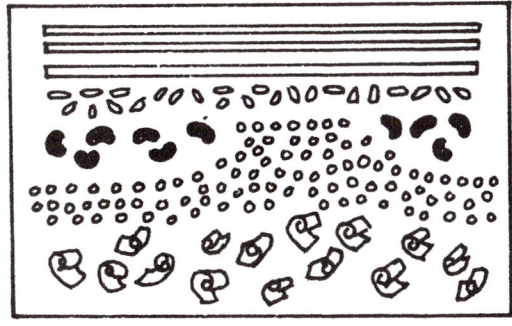

An alternative is to save jar lids, fill them with plasticine, and stick seeds into the plasticine.

Transform mosaic patterns into intriguing works of art by spraying with gold lacquer.

## Ceiling tile designs

Borrow some tacks, drawing pins, or brass studs from the woodwork corner. Provide a large, shallow box of assorted buttons. The children can hammer the tacks through the holes in the buttons, into polystyrene ceiling tiles. Place a board underneath to protect the table top. If you don't have enough hammers, tacks can be pressed in with the fingers. Later, the tacks can be pulled out ready for making fresh designs another day.

## TO FOLLOW UP

### Potato bash

Provide little boys and girls who are not quite ready for woodwork with large, washed potatoes, large-headed nails and hammers. Potatoes offer just the right amount of resistance. At the end of the hammering session you can retrieve the nails, but be sure to throw the potatoes away.

### Greeting card jig-saws

Cut the front pictures off greeting cards. Cut them in half. Mix them up. See if the children can match the right top and bottom halves.

### Where does it live ?

Save the plain backs of greeting cards. Cut them in half. On the top half draw or trace an animal, bird, insect, fish or plant. On the bottom half draw where it would live, for example, cat/basket, mouse/hole, bird/nest, bee/hive, fish/pond, flower/flower bed, boy and girl/house. Print the names in black ink using lower case letters. Mix the cards up and see if the children can match the tops and bottoms correctly.

# AUGUST week 2

## TO TALK ABOUT

### August holidays

August is a very popular month for holidays. Lots of people are travelling to and from their holidays in many different ways.

Sometimes a fair is held on the local green on August bank holiday, the last Monday in August. Travelling fair people seem to be the only ones who work on August bank holiday.

Even if the children in your group are not going on holiday or to a fair, they can experience some of the excitement in play. Look through a picture book with them that shows holiday scenes or fair scenes. Have any of the children been to a fair? Have any of them been away from home on holiday? What details can they remember? How did they travel? Can anybody bring souvenirs to show?

## TO LOOK FOR

### Fruit in the shops now

Apricots, cantaloup, watermelon, cherries, black-currants, figs, gooseberries, greengages, loganberries, peaches, pears, plums, raspberries, whortleberry (blueberry, bilberry), strawberries, grapes

## TO JOIN IN

### Cherry stone chant

When the children have been eating cherries, count the pile of stones each leaves to arrive at 'whom they are going to marry'. You can also count out on the number of buttons on their clothes.

'Tinker, tailor, soldier, sailor, richman, poor man, beggar man, thief, doctor, lawyer, Indian chief.' When you come to the end, begin again.

Another counting rhyme:

Two, four, six, eight,
Mary at the cottage gate,
Eating cherries off a plate,
Two, four, six, eight.

## Songs

*At the fair*

'Oh, dear, what can the matter be, Johnny's so long at the fair' (THE OXFORD NURSERY SONG BOOK)

We went to the animals' fair,
The birds and beasts were there,
The big baboon by the light of the moon,
Was combing his auburn hair.
The monkey he got drunk,
He sat on the elephant's trunk.
The elephant sneezed and caused a breeze,
And what became of the monk?

*Getting there*

'I'll take you riding in my car' (words in BBC book, PLAY SCHOOL PLAY IDEAS)
'We're going to the zoo, zoo, zoo' (MFP 7" record)
and

Down by the station early in the morning
See the little puffa-trains all in a row
Man in the engine pulls a little handle,
Puff, puff, toot-toot, off we go!

(Music in THIS LITTLE PUFFIN)

## Nursery rhyme

Simple Simon (full-length version in THE PUFFIN BOOK OF NURSERY RHYMES)

## Stories

'Jack and the Beanstalk'
'Stand back,' said the elephant, 'I'm going to sneeze,' by Patricia Thomas (World's Work)

## Poem

*The Holiday Train*

1 Here is the train!
Here is the train!
Let us get in!
Let us get in!

2 Where shall we sit?
Where shall we sit?
When will it go?
When will it go?

3 What does it say?
What does it say?
'Let us get on!'
'Let us get on!'

4 Look at the trees!
Look at the trees!
See all the cows!
See all the cows!

5 Isn't it fun?
  Isn't it fun?
  Going along!
  Going along!

6 Hurrying on!
  Hurrying on!
  Nearly there!
  Nearly there!

7 Look at the sea!
  Look at the sea!
  See all the ships!
  See all the ships!

8 Here we are!
  Here we are!
  Out we get!
  Out we get!
                    Irene Thompson

## Movement

Play trains. The adult in front is the engine. Children line up behind. Sing 'Down by the station, early in the morning' first, to get in the mood. Then move off, all making shunting movements with arms, like the links on the train wheels. Chant 'The Holiday Train' as you move around the room.

## TO INVESTIGATE

### Travelling

Set out the props for playing at travelling. A line of large cardboard grocery cartons with doors cut out could be a train. Place it between a home corner and a holiday corner. The holiday corner could be a kind of fair. Planks and chairs could be used to make an exciting run-up to the slippery slide. Make sure the planks are firm and low so that if there are any tumbles no one will get hurt. Help the little ones to keep their balance.

A game of skittles can be made out of liquid detergent bottles anchored to the floor with plasticine. Use a large, soft beach-ball to knock them down.

The children might look for pictures of different forms of travel in magazines to paste into a scrapbook or put on a pin board. Organisations like the Post Office are sometimes able to help with posters.

## TO CREATE

### Travel pictures

The children might like to draw their own versions of different forms of travel with chunky crayons. Help them to print what their creation is called, if it has a name. Sound out the spelling, using the sound that the letter makes, as well as naming the letter.

### A matchbox goods train

The engine is made with one matchbox plus an extra tray.

1  Push the tray three-quarters of the way out of the sleeve.
2  Insert the extra tray inside the pushed-out tray, facing away from the sleeve.
3  More trays can be added at the back for goods wagons. Use matchbox sleeves to join trays, or thread them together using a darning needle and button thread.

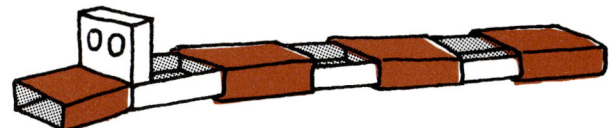

### A travel chart

If a road passes your playgroup, count with the children how many cars, how many lorries, how many buses, etc., pass in a ten minute period. Make a picture chart, drawing in the different vehicles.

## TO FOLLOW UP

### Visits

Short visits can be just as exciting as long holidays. When you go for walks with the children, look for the practical side of marvels we take for granted. Point out Post Office cables, manhole covers on drains, gas storage tanks, a reservoir. Wait for the postman to empty a pillar box (the notice on the box will tell you when he is due). Children give you a good excuse for standing and watching the rubbish truck grind up the rubbish. A trip to a rubbish dump is a highlight.

Ask your milkman where his milk and eggs come from. There might be a farm closer than you think where you and the children would be welcome. Have you been in touch with the local authority's safety officer yet for a talk on road safety?

### Keep a record

Children love to bring back postcards to remind them of a visit. Those they can bear to part with can be pasted in a scrapbook. Print the child's name and a few details underneath each postcard. Keep the book handy for children to browse through when the mood takes them.

# AUGUST week 3

## TO TALK ABOUT

### Harvest time

At this time of year the corn is harvested. Have the children noticed fresh corn cobs for sale at the greengrocer's? Sometimes the golden silky tassel is still attached. Perhaps someone could bring a corn cob to show. Wash it and break off a few pieces. Some of the children might like to gnaw a piece. Parrots like raw corn, and so do mice. People prefer cobs boiled and buttered.

Corn can be processed into corn flakes for breakfast, or ground up into cornflour for thickening soups and gravy.

### Corn dollies

Weaving corn dollies is a country craft. Besides dolly shapes there are many traditional designs into which corn stalks can be woven. They are often used as wall decorations. Perhaps somebody you know has one that you could borrow for the children to look at.

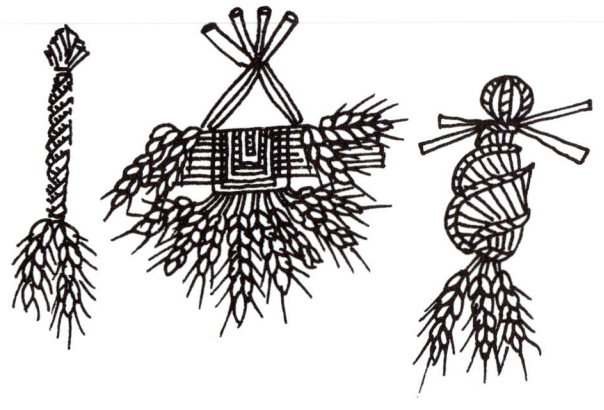

## TO LOOK FOR

### Plant life

Thistles, docks, ragwort, sunflower, sea poppy, marsh mallow, red poppies grow in cornfields that are ripe for harvesting; heather on hills; acorns appear on oak trees; rowan tree berries redden; yellow and brown leaves on elm and beech trees; water lilies; fuchsia; cactus; everlasting daisies

## TO JOIN IN

### Songs

Old MacDonald had a farm, Ee-I, Ee-I, O.
And on that farm he had some cows, Ee-I, Ee-I, O.
With a moo here, and a moo there,
Here a moo, there a moo,
Everywhere a moo, moo,
Old MacDonald had a farm, Ee-I, Ee-I, O.

Continue with other animals.

(Music in THE PUFFIN SONG BOOK and on an MFP 7″ record)

I went to visit a farm one day,
I saw the sheep across the way,
And this is what I heard them say, Baa, Baa.

Continue with other animals.

Jump down, spin around,
Pick a bale of cotton.
Jump down, spin around,
Pick a bale of hay.

(Begin slowly, singing and doing the actions. Repeat it, getting faster and faster.)

### Nursery stories

'The House That Jack Built'
'The Three Little Pigs'
'The Three Billy Goats Gruff'

## TO INVESTIGATE

### Making popcorn

Many delicatessen shops sell packets of special popping corn. If you have the use of a hot plate, pop some corn in a saucepan and season with butter and salt. The children will find it has a pleasant, savoury taste. Let them compare it with bought, sugared popcorn. Talk about the difference to stimulate language development. Compare it with breakfast cornflakes, brought to taste. Buy a sweet corn cob from the greengrocer's. Let the children taste the pieces raw, then boiled. Talk about the difference in texture and flavour. Add butter, salt and pepper to improve the flavour.

## Preserving grasses

August is a good time to gather attractive tall grasses. It is a bit like harvesting. Hang bunches upside down in a warm, dry place for several weeks. Then they can be used for flower arrangements, to sell at fund-raising functions, and for the children to give as Christmas presents. 'Honesty' grass must be peeled on each side to reveal the silver moons, which are everlasting. Can you obtain a cotton boll for the children to look at?

## TO CREATE

### A felt board farm

(Instructions in 'Things for adults to make')

A large square of black felt pasted to strong cardboard and farm animal shapes cut out of coloured felt will encourage children to make up their own stories and act them out with the animals.

### Straw beads

Cut hollow natural straw and coloured plastic drinking straws into short lengths for the children to thread into necklaces. They might like to add washed and pressed milk bottle tops.

### An orange pomander

Now is the time to prepare some small oranges for pomander Christmas presents. Let the children stick cloves into the orange all around. You will have to tie some strong, pretty thread around the orange, as if it were a parcel. Finish off at the top with a good loop. Hang the oranges in an airing cupboard to preserve them.

**A magic palm tree** (for you to make for the children)

1  Take two sheets of newspaper, one inside the other. Roll lengthways.
2  Holding the roll at the bottom, cut the top into fronds about 10 cm (4″) long.
3  Find the inside edge of the newspaper where you have been cutting. Pull it upwards obliquely, with a rolling movement until you have tiers of fronds going down your tree trunk.
4  Sticky-tape the roll firmly at the edge of the bottom tier.

## TO FOLLOW UP

### Hens and chickens

This game requires the participation of two adults, one to be the mother hen, one to be a fox. The children are chickens. The mother hen has to guard her train of chickens, who hang on behind her with arms around each other's waists, from the fox, who is intent on catching a plump chicken for dinner. The mother hen moves around with arms outstretched as the fox darts from one side to the other. If the fox touches a chicken, that chicken has to leave the mother hen and hang on behind the fox. The game continues until all the chickens are caught, or the children tire.

# AUGUST week 4

## TO TALK ABOUT

### How far can you see?

Have the children seen the man in the moon at night? Sometimes there seems to be a face there although an astronaut would tell you that it is mountain ranges and craters you can see. You really can see for billions of kilometres when you look up at the moon and stars. Nobody can see so far looking in any other direction.

Bring binoculars or a telescope for the children to look through. Things far away seem closer and look larger. Now let the children look through the wrong end of a telescope. Close things look small and seem further away.

Look at some photographs and illustrations with the children. Notice how people or objects in the foreground look large and things in the background look small. The same sort of thing happens with noise. The closer it is, the louder it seems; the further away it is, the softer it sounds.

## TO LOOK FOR

### Wildlife

Some birds, like the cuckoo, migrate; cocoons of emperor moth cling to heather like white silk.

### Weather

Hot, thunderstorms. Check thermometer. The last week of August heralds the arrival of autumn. Nature is at its most beautiful now. Leaves begin to turn red and brown on the trees. The full moon in August seems particularly bright. Farmers make good use of its light to extend the harvesting and it is called the harvest moon. Sometimes the moon looks like a bright new silver coin. Sometimes it is gold or orange. Sometimes you can see shooting stars in the autumn night sky.

## TO JOIN IN

### Movement

Here is a rhyme that illustrates how distance alters what we see and what we hear. You could say it to the children first, using 'I' instead of 'we'. Say the first two lines standing close. Go to the other end of the room to say the last two lines in each verse. Then the children can do it. Alternatively, instead of moving, they can stay where they are, and express the differences with their voices and actions.

When we are near,
A whisper may be heard.
When we are far,
We must shout every word.

When we are near,
We look giant size.
When we are far,
We shrink before your eyes.
(I.C.)

Shake a paper bag full of dry fallen leaves near and then far.

### Nursery rhymes

'Three blind mice'
'Hey diddle, diddle, the cat and the fiddle'
'Girls and boys come out to play'
'Six little mice sat down to spin'

The little mouse doth skip and play.
He runs by night and sleeps by day.

(All in THE PUFFIN BOOK OF NURSERY RHYMES)

### Action rhyme

A little mouse hid in a hole (one hand inside other)
Softly in a hole—
When all was quiet as could be—
Out popped he!

### A folk story

*The little field mice*

All the time the corn has been growing, little field mice have been building their nests and raising their families among the tall stalks. At harvest time they scamper for safety as their nests are cut down. There is a story about a field mouse family who overheard the farmer say to his wife, 'It is time to harvest our corn. Tomorrow I will ask the neighbours to help me cut it and gather it.'

The baby mice were frightened and asked their mother if they should move house at once. 'Not yet, my darlings,' she said. 'There's plenty of time.'

The next day they heard the farmer say to his wife, 'The neighbours are too busy cutting their own corn to help us. Tomorrow I will ask my brother and cousin to help me cut and gather my corn.' Once again the baby mice grew anxious, but their mother reassured them. The next day they heard the farmer say, 'My brother and cousin are too busy to help us. Tomorrow I will cut the corn and gather it myself.'

'Now is the time to move, my darlings,' said mother field mouse, 'for as you and the farmer have learned, the only way to get something done is not to depend on others, but to do it yourself.'

## TO INVESTIGATE

### Through a glass, safely

Some insects begin to grow drowsy and die in autumn. As bees grow slower they can be more easily caught in the hands by small children, or accidently trodden on by bare feet, so watch for the hazard of stings. Dead bees, wasps, dragonflies, blue-bottles or anything else that may be fascinating to look at but unpleasant for the children to handle, could be scooped into a glass jar or, better still, a clear plastic yogurt or jam pot, so that it may be examined on all sides with safety.

### A loudspeaker

A telescope makes far things seem close. A megaphone can be used as a loudspeaker or an ear trumpet. Here is how to make one.

1 Take a large square of stiff paper. Place it flat on a board to protect your table top.
2 Take a piece of string the length of your paper. Tie a drawing pin to one end, a pencil to the other.
3 Press the drawing pin into one corner of your paper. Then, holding the pencil straight, draw a curve from the bottom corner to the diagonally opposite corner.
4 Cut along the drawn line.
5 Curve the paper into a cone shape.
6 Sticky-tape the side edges together. Cut a little off the sharp end for a mouthpiece.

Prepare a sheet of paper to stage 3 for each child in advance. Show them how you did it. Help them to cut, shape and tape their cones.

When used the right way round, a megaphone seems to make a shout travel further. When used the wrong way round, it muffles sound. Ask the children to describe what happens when they use their cones as ear trumpets the right way round and then the wrong way. What happens with a cone over each ear?

## TO CREATE

### Moonmen

Here is a basic idea that can be taken several steps further according to the abilities of the children. The older ones who finish first can try another version so that they don't become bored.

Using a plate or biscuit tin as a pattern, trace a quantity of circles on stiff paper. The children can cut them out. As the moon is silver or gold, have some silver and gold paper for them to cut or tear up and stick on the circle with glue, just for fun. Has anybody made a pattern that could look like a man in the moon?

Show the children how to make a reversible happy/sad face in a circle—one that you can turn upside down. Have plenty of circles ready for the children who wish to experiment with this idea.

Some of the children might like to try cutting holes for eyes and mouth to make a mask.

## TO FOLLOW UP

Megaphone shapes made in black become witches' hats.

The children could help you to make a witch's broom for sweeping up the autumn leaves. Look among the twigs that the wind blows down for a long, strong stick. That can be the handle. Gather twigs, strip off the leaves, and bind them tightly with twine in layers around the handle.

### Womble masks

Make a cone shape in stiff black paper. Cut out two eye holes. Cut away a little of the rim to fit under a child's chin.

The children can glue on little pieces of material or paper to make a furry texture. Try using two toning colours like brown and orange. Leave the end of the nose black. Fasten around the back of the head with hat elastic. Womble masks are a great inducement to tidy up the garden.

### Look at

SIZE, Macdonald First Library

# SEPTEMBER week 1

## TO TALK ABOUT

### Precious stones

Have you any costume jewellery set with coloured stones that you could show to the children as a talking point? Some mothers who have jewelled rings might like to stay to talk about the stones set in them. Perhaps an adult could loan some polished and unpolished semi-precious stones for the children to handle. What other sorts of stones do we value?

Slate is a stone used for roofing tiles. Marble, sandstone and granite are used for building. Ordinary rough stones can be used to build a fence. Are there any farm fences like this nearby? Gravel is used in making roads. Pebbles are used for paths. You might find a cobbled street illustrated in a picture book.

Look for interesting shapes and colours in stones in the garden, and when you go on walks. Look for ways in which stone has been used in your neighbourhood. Look for stones worn smooth at the seaside and try to guess what kind they are.

You don't have to own a tumble polishing kit to make semi-precious stones shine. Spread all the stones the children gather on a sheet of newspaper and spray them with clear varnish to make them special.

## TO LOOK FOR

### Gold for the colour table

Gold is a metal sometimes found in rocks. It is also a colour. Wedding rings are usually gold. New pennies and polished brass and copper objects look golden. Sand, sunshine and ripening corn look golden. Hair can be the colour of gold. Brocade sometimes has gold thread in it. You can buy lacy gold paper doilies for parties.

Some chocolates are wrapped in gold paper. Rub it with your fingers to make it thin and tinselly. The children might like to smooth out tinsel papers and take them home to place between the pages of a favourite book. It makes a nice surprise to come across when they look through the pages. Maybe when they are grown up and have children of their own, the tinsel might be discovered by their little children.

What other gold or gilt things can you find for the colour table?

## TO JOIN IN

### Movement

Provide a treasure chest full of old bits of costume jewellery and beads for a special dressing-up session.

Have a treasure hunt for a cardboard chest containing chocolate coins in gold paper for all to share.

### Nursery songs

'I had a little nut tree'
'London bridge is falling down'

(Music in THE PUFFIN SONG BOOK)

### Poem

*Precious Stones*

An emerald is as green as grass,
A ruby red as blood;
A sapphire shines as blue as heaven,
A flint lies in the mud.

A diamond is a brilliant stone,
To catch the world's desire.
An opal holds a fiery spark,
But a flint holds fire.

Christina Rossetti

### Story

THE SUN BOX, English text by Antonia Ridge (Harrap)

## TO INVESTIGATE

### Golden pennies

The children will enjoy shining old pennies to make them look like gold. Polish-impregnated wadding is less messy to use than liquid polish. Rub over with a soft, dry cloth to bring up the shine. (If you have any coins that you suspect might be collector's pieces, don't polish them as it may lower their value.)

Sitting at a table, hold a coin on edge with the index finger of the left hand. Flick one side with the thumb and middle finger of the right hand to make it spin.

Make a fist and place the penny on top. Flick it up

with your thumb. Can the children guess whether it will come down heads or tails?

## Penny magic

*Pushing a penny through the table*

Keep a penny up the sleeve of your left arm. Hold up a penny in your right hand for the children to see. Put the penny in your fist and pretend to push it through the table with a rubbing motion, into the left hand waiting to catch it underneath. Slip the right-hand penny up your sleeve. Slip the left-hand penny down into your hand, and the trick is complete.

*The disappearing penny*

Tell the children that you can make a penny disappear into thin air, and reappear on somebody's head. Have one penny in your right hand, and another one up your left sleeve. Wave the visible penny in the air, slip it down your sleeve without the children noticing, and pretend it has disappeared. Put the left hand down to touch a child on the head. The hidden penny will slip down the sleeve into your hand and seem to be picked up from the child's head by magic.

## TO CREATE

### Plasticine finery

Provide plasticine and show the children how to roll it to make rings, bracelets and necklaces. Explain to them that the ball of plasticine has not become more in quantity when it has been rolled long and thin. Demonstrate in different ways how the shape can change while the amount remains the same.

### Paper beads

You will need a pencil for each child, a saucer of water, some coloured gummed paper squares cut into strips, and a jar of vaseline.

The children should coat their pencils with vaseline to stop the gum sticking. Next they wet the gummed paper and wind the strip around the pencil. Slip the strip off the end of the pencil and leave to dry into a bead shape for threading.

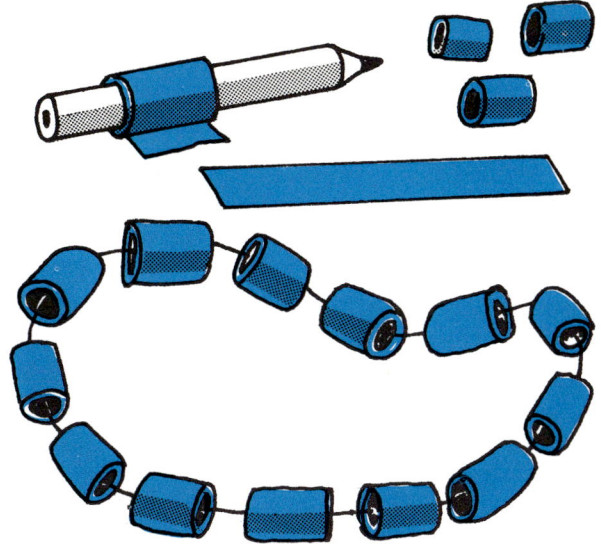

### Crown jewels

Cut crowns in the usual way out of strong gold paper. Buy a box of clear, coloured plastic jewel shapes for the children to stick on. Shiny gems can also be made by gluing coloured cellophane to aluminium kitchen foil. Talk about the distinctive colours of jewels as they are glued on. What would a red stone be called? What might a sparkling, colourless one be? What colour is an emerald?

## TO FOLLOW UP

### Stepping stones

Stepping stones are very useful stones. They can be quite ordinary, not precious at all, just as long as they are large enough to put a foot on, close enough together and high enough out of the water so that we can walk across a stream on them and not get our feet wet.

Cut large 'stepping stones' out of strong paper, and place them in a path across the room. Make a game of trying to walk on them without wobbling off.

### Pebble animals

Save smooth pebbles from the beach, and other interestingly-shaped stones for the children to glue together to make simple animal shapes. For instance, a stone and a piece of string for a tail make a mouse; a large stone and five small ones can be made into a tortoise. Use strong impact adhesive. Wax polish will make pebble sculptures shine.

### Look at

ROCKS AND MINERALS, Macdonald Junior Reference Library

THE STORY OF OUR ROCKS AND MINERALS, A Ladybird Nature Book

# SEPTEMBER week 2

## TO TALK ABOUT

### You've got rhythm

There is rhythm in speech, just as there is in music. For instance, if one of the children in your group is called Susan, there is a strong and a light beat in her name. Jonathan has a strong, a light, and a strong beat in his name. Go around the circle clapping out the rhythm of each child's name. When you are filling in the attendance register, clap out each name. Each child claps out the reply 'I am here'.

Go around the circle again, asking each child what he or she had for breakfast. All together clap out the rhythm of what each child had. Think of other phrases with interesting rhythms that you and the children can clap out.

## TO LOOK FOR

### Fruit in the shops now

Apples, blackberries, cantaloup, watermelon, figs, pears, plums

## TO JOIN IN

### Action song

*Let's all clap together*

Let's all clap together,
Clap together,
Let's all clap together,
Clap, clap, clap!
Clap, clap this-a-way, (turn to neighbour on left)
Clap, clap that-a-way, (turn to neighbour on right)
Clap, clap, all the day,
Clap, clap, clap.

Continue with:

Let's all tap together (with feet)
Let's all shout together (hands cupped to lips)
Let's all whisper together (finger on lips)

Oh, we can play on the triangle
And this is the music to it—
Ting ting ting ting ting ting ting
And that's the way we do it!

(Music in THIS LITTLE PUFFIN)

Give every child a chance to play his or her instrument solo, then put all the sounds together for the last verse.

## TO INVESTIGATE

### Sound effects

Experiment with sound effects such as shaking a box of beads or shaking sand through a sieve onto newspaper to make a noise like rain. Wobble hardboard for thunder. The clip, clop of two coconut halves or two small plant pots sounds like a horse's hooves.

Other interesting noises are the rustle of dry leaves being shaken in a paper bag, drumming with the fingers on a table top, clicking the fingers, clicking your tongue against the roof of your mouth to make another sort of galloping sound, hitting a horseshoe with a nail, humming with the lips vibrating against tissue paper held across a comb, making animal noises into a kazoo, humming through a toilet roll tube and breaking up the sound by tapping your fingers across the end where the sound comes out, tapping your lips with your fingers, wobbling your bottom lip with your index finger as you hum, patting your hand over your open mouth to give an Indian war whoop, the spring of comb teeth as you run your fingers along the top edge, the echo of a galvanised iron bucket or oil drum, the clang of saucepan lid cymbals, and the bang of a wooden spoon on a saucepan drum.

## TO CREATE

### Home-made instruments (for you to make for the children)

*Drums*

Old rubber gloves are a handy source of drum rubber. Cut off the wrist to give yourself a wide rubber band.

Cut the glove open down one side and across fingers and thumb to obtain a large flat piece of rubber. Stretch it across a paint tin. Stretch the rubber band over it to keep it in place. With a darning needle, thread string evenly all around between rubber and a curtain ring held under the tin to keep the rubber taut. Smooth the ends of pieces of dowelling with sandpaper to make drum sticks. You can force cotton reels onto the ends to make more noise. For a softer sound, buy a washing-up mop and sew the mop head into a firm ball. Old chamois leathers can also be used for drum or tambourine skins.

*Shakers*

Liquid detergent containers can be part-filled with dried beans and the opening jammed with a dowelling handle for shaking. Attach securely, using padding and woodwork glue if necessary.

Most home-made instruments look better for a little painting and decorating. Some small size plastic scouring powder pots merely need a circle of cardboard glued over the pouring holes.

*A guitar*

Use a date box or cigar box with a lid. Make nicks in the ends of the box, and cut a hole in the lid. Slice a cork in half lengthways and glue one half just above the hole in the lid. Stretch rubber bands around the box for guitar strings, fitting them in the nicks and over the cork.

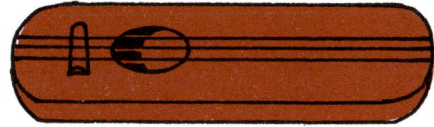

*Jingle bells*

Sew tin bells on pieces of ribbon or not-too-tight elastic bracelets.

*Rhythm sticks*

Saw lengths of bamboo for rhythm sticks to bang together. New carpets often come rolled around a stout length of bamboo, which is ideal for rhythm sticks.

*Wind instruments*

Whistles, trumpets and flutes should be used with discretion. They can spread infection from mouth to mouth. Also, children might trip and cut their lips on the instruments.

**TO FOLLOW UP**

Set up a noise corner. With string, hang saucepans, lids, spoons, etc., on a clothes-horse for free experimentation.

If you can borrow a tape recorder, tape some of the sound effects and music you and the children create, and play it back to them.

**Telephones**

Make telephones by piercing a hole in the bottom of two clean yogurt pots, tins or plastic margarine tubs, and threading a length of string between them. Knot firmly at both ends. When two children hold the string taut between them, they will be able to talk into one container, and listen with the other alternately. Margarine tubs make the best telephones, as the wide, flimsy base vibrates, making a sensitive diaphragm for reproducing sounds.

**Instruments for children to make**

*An electric guitar*

If the children have been watching you improvise instruments, they will want to make instruments too. Have a collection of junk tins and boxes ready. Make sure that the tins have no sharp edges. A little boy amazed me by gluing a narrow kitchen foil box to a paper tissues box that had an oblong hole for pulling out tissues. The result was a guitar. I found some large elastic bands to stretch around the tissue box for strings. He attached string with a square of plasticine on the end, which he stuck to the wall for an electric plug. A little girl wandered around singing into a skipping rope microphone.

*Shakers*

Provide plastic pots with fitting lids, such as those used for cottage cheese. Set out saucers of buttons, rice, pasta, seeds, dried beans. Let the children experiment with the different sounds these things make when shaken in the plastic pots.

# SEPTEMBER week 3

## TO TALK ABOUT

### Thanksgiving

In late September or early October we celebrate Harvest Festival. At this joyous church service we thank God for the harvest and all the good things we have to eat through the year. You could explain to the children how city people, as well as farmers, take offerings of food to church to be given to people who are less well off.

Many playgroups owe their existence to church halls. This is an ideal time to say 'thank you' by visiting the church with the children and taking an offering, at a time that suits the vicar. A bunch of Michaelmas daisies would help to decorate the church. Apples or blackberries might be available for the picking in somebody's garden. You might even try baking a few loaves of home-made bread to take, saving a loaf for the children to sample.

Give the children time to absorb the atmosphere of the church; to look at the stained glass windows, flickering candles, rich wood, shadowy corners, and gargoyles. When you talk about it with them afterwards, you might be surprised how observant they are about church architecture outside as well as inside. Watch for some of these themes being expressed in the children's paintings.

## TO LOOK FOR

### Plant life

Michaelmas daisies, mushrooms, the Aspen tree quivers, barley harvest time, beech tree leaves turn pale yellow to bronze, spindleberry, horse chestnuts, Spanish chestnuts, acorns drop their little 'elfin caps'.

Many deciduous trees start to shed their leaves. Trees that keep their leaves all winter are called evergreens. Look for different leaf shapes and leaf edgings. Notice the palmate leaves of the horse chestnut, shaped rather like the palm of a hand with fingers. Look for the horseshoe-shaped scars on the main trunk where low branches have been shed as the tree grew. Collect fallen pine cones for Christmas decorations. You could spray some gold. Can you find any with the seeds still in them? The birds like these. You may see pine resin on the pine tree bark. It has a lovely fresh smell.

## TO JOIN IN

### Acting out song

(Music in THIS LITTLE PUFFIN)

There was a princess long ago,
Long ago, long ago.
There was a princess long ago,
long ago.
   (A child is chosen to be princess. She stands in the centre of a ring of children.)

And she lived in a big, high tower,
   (Children raise their joined hands to make the tower.)

One day a fairy waved her wand,
   (A child chosen to be fairy waves her arm over princess.)

The princess slept for a hundred years,
   (Princess lies down and closes her eyes.)

A great big forest grew around,
   (Children wave their arms as trees.)

A gallant prince came riding by,
   (Child chosen to be prince gallops round the outside of ring.)

He drew his sword and cut it down,
   (Prince pretends to cut down trees.)

He took her hand to wake her up,
   (He wakes up princess.)

So everybody's happy now,
Happy now, happy now.
So everybody's happy now,
Happy now.
   (Children skip round clapping their hands.)

If you sing this often, make an effort to see that every child has a turn at being a princess and a prince and you will satisfy many secret longings. Another favourite song of this type is 'Oh soldier, soldier, won't you marry me?' (in THE PUFFIN SONG BOOK).

### Story

Look for the simplest storybook version of 'The Sleeping Beauty' at your library.

### Finger-play rhyme

Here's the church     (fingers interlaced and arched,
                    thumb-tips touching)
Here's the steeple (raise two index fingers together)
Open the doors    (open thumbs, turn fingers 'inside
                       out')

And here are the people! (wiggle fingers).

## TO INVESTIGATE

### Growing a lot of cress in a little space

The children might like to grow and harvest their own watercress. Here's how to give each a little plot in which to take an interest. First obtain a paper pulp egg tray from a grocer's or market stall. When you use eggs, save the shells. Wash them and half-fill each with cotton wool. With felt pens, print a child's name on each shell. The children might like to draw a face on the shell too. Place the shells in the tray. Sprinkle on cress seeds. Water. Keep in a dark place until the seeds germinate, then place in a light, sunny position. Keep the cotton wool moist. When the cress has grown, the children can cut it with scissors, like hair, and eat it in small, dainty sandwiches.

### Carrot tops

Place a carrot top in a saucer of water. In a few days it will sprout green fronds.

## TO CREATE

### Conker chairs (for you to make for the children)

As pins are used, this is a little bit dangerous for the youngest children to try themselves, but they will enjoy watching you make doll's house furniture out of horse chestnuts. Make sure no pins go astray.

Conkers are not as hard as they look. Press four pins into the bottom of one for chair legs. Stick another four pins half-way round the top. That is the frame for a woven back. Tie a length of wool to the end pin, and weave it in and out of the four pins until you have filled in the back. A conker with four pin legs and no back could be a stool or a table. Slices of cork can be used in the same way.

### Matchbox furniture

Even the youngest children can enjoy gluing two matchboxes together to make a chest of drawers for the doll's house. What other furniture designs can you and the children create? Wrapping doll's house dolls in scraps of material for clothes makes another quietly satisfying session.

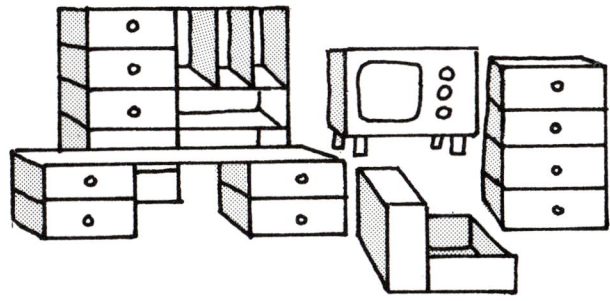

## TO FOLLOW UP

### Pine cone weatherman

Have you noticed that pine cones open when the weather is dry, and close up when it starts to rain? If you find an open cone and place it in water, it will close up tight in an hour or so. Place it near a radiator and it will open again.

The children can make pine cones into weather men by adding a paper ball, cottonwool ball, or plasticine head, and pipe cleaner arms. Make a plasticine base.

### Look at

WHAT TO LOOK FOR IN AUTUMN (Ladybird Nature Book), will tell you more about mushrooms in particular.
WHAT TO LOOK FOR IN CHURCH (Ladybird)

## TO TALK ABOUT

### Making pictures

From the library select some picture books that use simple, and some that use unusual, art techniques. Show the pictures to the children and ask if they can guess how each picture was done. It might be a photographed collage, pen and wash, crayon, or scraper board technique. Talk about the different ways of doing things. Which techniques particularly appeal to the children? Which do they like the least? Do they prefer lots of colour or black and white? Don't worry about not knowing technical terms; the important point is that there are lots of exciting ways of composing a picture. You don't have to stick to brushing paint on paper. Wouldn't it be fun to explore other possibilities?

## TO LOOK FOR

### Wildlife

Wasps hum drowsily, spiders spin webs in garden, squirrels hide nuts, field mice hide grain, all wild creatures prepare for winter. Garden snails sleep in huddles under a stone or in a crack of the garden wall.

### Weather

Some sunny, hot days; early morning mists, chilly evenings. Check thermometer.

## TO JOIN IN

### Movement

*A slow race*

A snail moves very slowly. Can the children move about as slowly as a snail? You could have a slow motion race over a short distance. The children have to keep moving, and the winner is the one who comes last. Then all have a run around to loosen up. You might like to time a fast race and a slow race with a stopwatch.

### Poems

'Mr Bidery's Spidery Garden,' by David McCord, from the PROVENSON BOOK OF FUN AND NONSENSE.

'Miss Polly had a dolly who was sick, sick, sick,' from THIS LITTLE PUFFIN.

## TO INVESTIGATE

### Action painting

Restrict action painting to four children at a time. Co-opt at least two extra helpers, one to watch the rest of the group and see that every child who wants to participate has a turn, and the other to supervise handwashing afterwards.

1 In a jug, mix powder paint with wallpaper paste to a medium-thick consistency. Pour into a plastic liquid detergent bottle and replace the squirting top.
2 Protect a large floor area with several layers of newspaper. Lay paper to be painted on well within the newspaper area. It could be end rolls from a newspaper printing office, background paper from a photographic studio, overlapping sheets of sugar paper, or more newsprint.
3 Place washable chairs on the newspaper for the children to operate from. Be prepared with lots of cloths for wiping up afterwards.
4 Cover the children as completely as possible in smocks. Remove shoes and socks systematically so that you know which are whose.

5 Children stand on chairs and squeeze paint from the squeezy bottles across the paper. Inevitably, they will want to get down from the chairs and get in close to their work. At that stage you could supply large sponges or blocks of foam rubber, paint rollers,

pastry cutters, biscuit tins for circle shapes and square shapes, potato cuts, brussels sprouts cut in half, leaves, feathers, combs, stiff cardboard with wedges cut out along one edge to make teeth to scrape through paint. Supply saucers of thicker paint if necessary. Paint rollers can be used with baking trays of paint.

Hands and feet make excellent templates. When you have recovered from cleaning up this mess, you might like to provide a long strip of paper, and let each child make a painty footprint. Print each child's name next to his mark. Do the same with hand prints. When dry, mount the strips on the wall with special display putty, or store them as scrolls.

## TO CREATE

### A composite height picture

How much have the children grown since you measured them in January? Lay a large piece of paper on the floor. Have each child in turn lie on the paper. Draw around them. Use a different coloured thick felt pen or crayon for each child. Print the name along each outline.

### A girl and boy chart

How many girls and how many boys are there in your group? The children could help you count. Rule a simple T shape on paper. Write 'girls' at the top of one column, 'boys' at the top of the other. Stick a square or doll shape of coloured gummed paper for each child in the appropriate columns. Print the number in pencil at the bottom. You may need to add to the squares, so leave the columns open.

## What makes a snail ?

Suggest that each child tries to create a snail, in any way he or she likes. It could be made of scraps from the junk play box, or of clay or plasticine. It could be a brush or a finger painting, a line drawing, or a collage. The creation could be one snail or a huddle of snails. It could be a snail in tall grass, or a pattern of snail trails.

## TO FOLLOW UP

### Cover-ups

One of the best cover-ups for messy play is made by cutting down the sleeves on an old blouse or shirt. If the sleeves are too wide for a child, continue the side seam up through the sleeve join, and stitch the sleeve narrower. Cut away the excess material with pinking shears. Make a hem at the bottom of the sleeves and thread elastic through for the child's wrists. The smock can be worn back-to-front to protect all of the child's clothes at the front.

Old white shirts cut down make good doctors' and nurses' uniforms. Detachable white collars, if you can get them, become nurses' caps. Thread elastic between the two collar stud holes.

### Icing demonstration

If one of the mothers is good at icing cakes, perhaps she could be persuaded to show the children how she pipes icing on a birthday cake for the dolls, or on plain biscuits. The principle is similar to squeezy bottle action painting, and is an interesting way to make three-dimensional patterns. Let the children spread icing on plain biscuits with a wet blunt knife and add 'hundreds and thousands' for decoration.

### Look at

SNAILS, by Eleanor Stodart (Angus & Robertson)

# OCTOBER    week 1

## TO TALK ABOUT

### Spider webs in the garden

One of the loveliest sights of autumn is a perfect spider web hung with morning dew glistening in the sun. Sometimes several webs are spun close together at different angles. The criss-crossed strands dazzle our eyes.

At ground level the children may see dozens of tiny, perfect webs spun between blades of grass, and outlined in frost. Have the children noticed any particularly beautiful, large or small spider webs recently? Perhaps there is one nearby that you could all look at.

## TO LOOK FOR

### Black for the colour table

Black is the night sky. Black is a hole in the ground or in a hollow tree. Black is the opposite of white.

Hair can be black. Horses and dogs can be black. Witches' hats and witches' cats are supposed to be black. Spiders, beetles and shoes can be black. Blackbirds, bats, and coal are black. Priests wear black. Printed words in books are black. Black can be velvety or shiny. What else can the children think of that is black?

## TO JOIN IN

### Movement

*A spider catching a fly*

Hold out your left hand, palm upwards, fingers outstretched, for the children to imitate. That is your spider's web. Rest the fingers of the right hand, grouped together like legs, in the centre of the left palm. That is your spider. Now imagine a fly has been caught by the web, on your left index finger. The 'spider' scrabbles out to wrap its prey up in web. Then it scrabbles back to the centre of the web again to wait for the next victim.

Now, imagine that your right hand is a big, tropical spider. It doesn't spin a web. It comes creeping out of a hole in the ground. It looks around with eyes on stalks (two fingers raised). It sees a big, tropical fly in front of it, and pounces!

Spiders are useful because they help to keep down the numbers of some insects that are pests.

### Game

Draw a line on the floor with chalk. Now, put your head down, one arm held in front like an elephant's trunk, one behind for a tail. Shuffle a few steps along the line as you sing this verse:

An elephant went out one day,
On a cobweb for to play.
He found it such tremendous fun,
He asked another elephant to come.

Continue with 'Two elephants went out one day', 'Three elephants', etc., until all the children have joined the elephant on the cobweb. Then shuffle round to make a circle with no beginning and no end. Finish with:

'All of a sudden the cobweb broke,
And down came all the elephant folk.'
(All fall on floor.)

### Action rhymes

Inksy Winksy spider, climbing up the spout,
Down came the rain and washed the spider out.
Out came the sunshine and dried up all the rain,
And Inksy Winksy spider climbed up the spout again.

Little Miss Muffet sat on her tuffet,
Eating her curds and whey.
Along came a spider who sat down beside her,
And frightened Miss Muffet away.

### Nursery songs

'I know an old lady who swallowed a fly', on CHILDREN'S FAVOURITES record MFP1175.
'The Spider and the Fly'. Music in THE OXFORD NURSERY SONG BOOK.

## TO INVESTIGATE

### Black as a background

Try to obtain some black cartridge paper for the children to draw on with white chalk. Coloured chalk also shows up well. Supply a saucer of water and let the children experiment with wet chalk.

Suggest that the children draw their idea of a white, frosty cobweb on the black background.

This might be a good opportunity to freshen up worn blackboards with a new coat of blackboard paint. If anybody has off-cuts of hardboard to spare, paint them with blackboard paint for the children to use as slates. A rectangle of carpet underlay glued to a small cardboard box makes a good blackboard duster.

If you have a paved concrete area outdoors for the children to play on, consider painting part of it with three coats of blackboard paint. It can be used for budding pavement artists to draw on with coloured chalks, for giant noughts and crosses, for drawing straight and wavy lines to walk along, for the floor of a make-believe house, and for seeing if everyone can fit on at the same time. The children can have fun cleaning off their drawings with a bucket of soapy water and a scrubbing brush.

## TO CREATE

### A spider

Cut a paper pulp egg box into cup sections, one for each child. The children can paint them black. When the paint is dry, make four holes near the rim on each side of each cup. Thread four furry black pipe cleaners through to make a spider's eight legs. (If the pipe cleaners are very long, cut them in half first.) The children can cut out circles of gummed paper and stick them on for eyes. Make two holes in the top and thread through black hat elastic. Knot the loop. Make a spare spider for yourself.

**A web** (for you to make for the children)
Take a sheet of hardboard. Cover with black paper and glue down flat. When dry, hammer in bayonet tacks, one at each corner and one in the middle of each side, making eight altogether. Take a ball of gold crocheting yarn. Tie the end to one of the tacks. Holding the thread taut, take it across the board to the opposite tack, round and on to the next one. Go around it and across to the opposite tack, and so on, until you have been round all the tacks. Knot all the threads together at the centre.

Unwind a good length of the thread from the ball, and cut. Knot the thread around one of the radiating threads a little way out from the centre. Go to the next thread, wind the thread around and knot. Continue this way until you arrive back at the radiating thread where you started. Go a little farther up this thread, and make a knot. Go over to the next thread, wind around and make a knot, and so on.

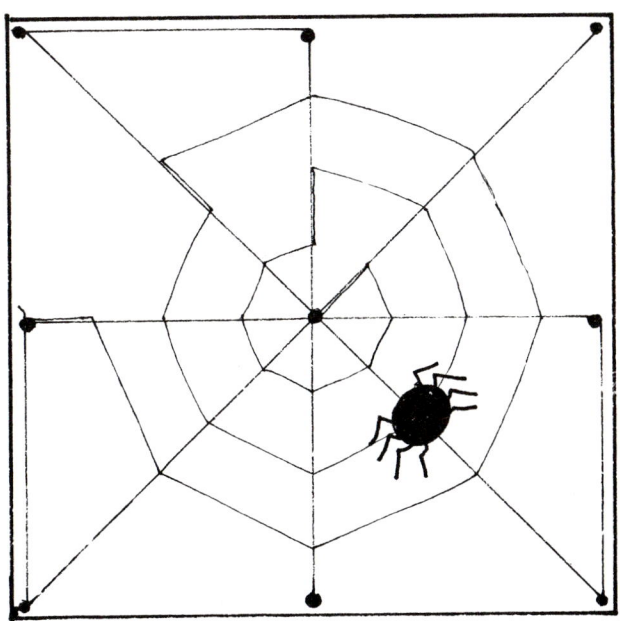

You only need to go around about four times to give the children the basic idea of a spider's web. Attach your spider to the web.

## TO FOLLOW UP

### Observation

If the children find something that looks like it might be a spider's egg sac, keep it in a covered jar with air holes in the lid until next year, when it might hatch into a lot of baby spiders.

Take another look at a real spider's web. How closely does it resemble the web you made? Can the children tell you what is the same about it? What is different?

## TO TALK ABOUT

### Jack Frost

Show the children a leaf with frost on it. Did they see any like that as they came to playgroup? Perhaps some of the children can find frosty leaves to bring in to show this week.

Was there frost on the bedroom windows when the children woke up? Is the frost deep enough yet to scrunch under your feet when you go for a morning walk? When the weather begins to get nippy, people say, 'Jack Frost is about. Watch out for your fingers and toes. He'll nip them with icy fingers.'

## TO LOOK FOR

### Fruit in the shops now

Apples, crab apples, avocado pears, blackberries, figs, oranges, pears, plums, melons, grapes.

## TO JOIN IN

### Movement

*Watch out! Jack Frost's about!*

Make 'nippy fingers' for the children. Cut out long, slim triangles of paper. Cut a slit near the base for the child's finger to go under the 'nail'. Sticky-tape them on if necessary.

Long fingernails help the creepy feeling. Now the children can tip-toe about, harmlessly nipping each other.

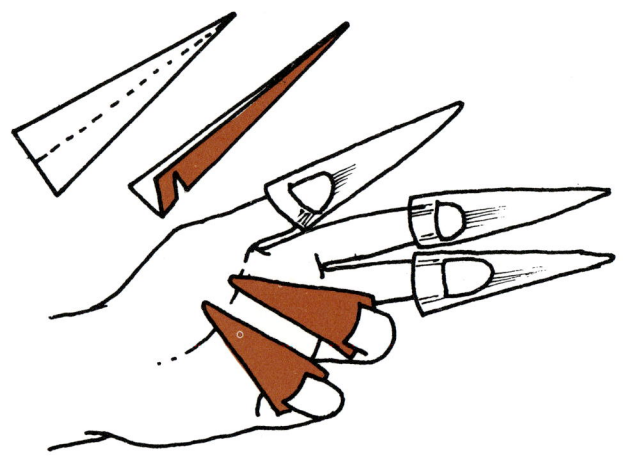

## Poems

### *Jack Frost*

The door was shut, as doors should be,
Before you went to bed last night;
But Jack Frost has got in, you see,
And left your window silver white.

He must have waited till you slept;
And not a single word he spoke,
But pencilled o'er the panes and crept
Away again before you woke.

And now you cannot see the hills
Nor fields that stretch beyond the lane
But there are fairer things than these
His fingers traced on every pane.

Rocks and castles towering high;
Hills and dales and streams and fields;
And knights in armour riding by,
With nodding plumes and shining shields.

And here are little boats, and there
Big ships with sails spread to the breeze;
And yonder, palm trees waving fair,
On islands set in silver seas.

And butterflies with gauzy wings;
And herds of cows and flocks of sheep
And fruit and flowers and all the things
You see when you are sound asleep.

For creeping softly underneath
The door, when all the lights are out,
Jack Frost takes every breath you breathe
And knows the things you think about.

He paints them on the window pane,
In fairy lines with frozen steam;
And when you wake you see again
The lovely things you saw in dream.
Gabriel Setoun

### *An Eskimo Baby*

If you were an Eskimo baby
You'd live in a bag all day.
 Right up from your toes
 To the tip of your nose,
All in thick cosy furs tucked away.

And if you went out for an airing
In mother's warm hood you would go,
    Tied close to her back
    Like a soft, furry pack,
You could laugh at the cold and the snow.

But if they brought water at bedtime—
As people at home always do—
    You'd cough and you'd sneeze,
    And perhaps you would freeze,
You would certainly turn very blue!

An Eskimo mummy would rub you
With oil from your heels to your head.
    And then you'd be rolled
    (For it's terribly cold)
In warm furs, and put safely to bed.

No nice creamy milk for your supper,
But bits of raw blubber and fat!
    Would you like to go
    To the land of the snow,
Where they have such a bedtime as that?
                    Lucy Diamond

## TO INVESTIGATE

### Frost patterns

Is there frost on the playgroup windows first thing in the morning? If there is, the children might like to draw patterns with their fingers before they take their gloves off. If there isn't any frost, the children could huff on the windows and draw where they have huffed.

Is it cold enough for the children to see their own breath making steam in the air? Have they noticed any horses going by, with steam coming from their nostrils like dragons, and steam rising off their bodies? What happens to the frost on leaves when they are brought indoors and warmed?

## TO CREATE

### Patterns like frost

Suggest that the children draw some frost patterns of their own. They will need a choice of special materials for this . . . white paper and soft lead pencils; black and white crayons; black paper and white chalk. Write down what they see in their patterns, if they would like you to.

## Totem poles

Save plastic yogurt pots. Remove printed labels with wire wool. Give each child a pot to make into a funny face. Place half the pots the right way up, and half upside down. Supply quick-drying glue, egg box noses and ears, cottonwool and straw packing hair, felt and gummed paper eyebrows, eyes, mouths, moustaches, and spare pieces for the children to cut up for themselves. Glue all the yogurt pot heads together to make some funny totem poles.

## TO FOLLOW UP

### Ice crystals

Make some ice cubes. Take them out of the freezer when they are half-frozen and put them on a tray for the children to investigate. The crystal formation is easily seen at this stage. Compare these with completely frozen cubes. Put an ice cube in the children's drinks so that they can feel and taste ice with their tongues.

Make floral ice cubes by freezing a flower inside. (If the ice cubes are going to be used in drinks, choose non-poisonous flowers, such as jasmine or violets.)

Can the children imagine what it must be like to see a great big iceberg in the ocean? To live in an ice igloo? Look for appropriate picture books at your library.

### An ice rink

Leave a shallow dish of water outdoors overnight to see if it will freeze. Use it as a skid pan for toy cars until it melts. Ice can be brought indoors to melt, then taken outdoors to freeze again. You can't do the same thing with snow. Isn't that interesting?

### Look at

HOT AS AN ICE CUBE, by Philip Balestrino, a 'Let's read and find out' book (A. & C. Black).

# OCTOBER week 3

## TO TALK ABOUT

### Pink and purple sunsets

The evening sky can be very beautiful at this time of year. Pink and purple clouds make a path to the setting sun. Have the children noticed this? Perhaps someone is wearing a pink shirt or a purple dress, which would remind them of the colours. There is a lot of colour in nature in the autumn. Pink berries on the spindle trees; purple crocus flowers; heaps of orange-brown leaves to plough through with your shoes. Try to bring some of the colours in nature into your room. Can the children think of anything they could bring?

## TO LOOK FOR

### Plant life

Michaelmas daisies, dying bracken, falling leaves, autumn crocus, hazelnuts, walnuts, chestnuts, conker nuts (horse chestnut), Cape gooseberries; clusters of orange berries appear on rowan trees, and pink (poisonous) berries on the spindle tree.

Plant hyacinth bulbs now for spring. Take cuttings for a cactus garden.

## TO JOIN IN

### Movement

Ask the children to pretend they are downy pink and purple clouds, gently scudding through the sky, blown by the breeze. Encourage them to explore all the space in the room. Then they can stand still and take deep breaths, pretending to draw more and more water up from the earth into their expanding bodies. Show the children how to draw up their arms as they feel themselves blowing up bigger and bigger. Now they can all shuffle in together to form one big, black solid rain cloud in the middle of the room. Some appropriate chords on the piano will help the threatening feeling. Then 'crash' on a tambourine for the downpour to begin. The children sink lower and lower as they lose all their rain, and end up relaxed on the floor.

Make silver swizzles to dance with and follow their twirly movements.

## Action song

*Ten Green Bottles,*
or as many bottles as you have children in your group.

There were ten green bottles a-standing on the wall,
Ten green bottles a-standing on the wall,
And if one green bottle should accidentally fall . . .
There'd be nine green bottles a-standing on the wall.

A line of children are the bottles. Watch how each in turn hams up the 'fall', collapsing on the floor.

## TO INVESTIGATE

### Colour mixing and merging

How many of the children have a spinning top? If all the tops were brought to playgroup on the same day, it would be quite spectacular trying to keep them all spinning at the same time. The children would be able to see how the different colours on the tops mix and merge when the spin begins. You can achieve the same effect with a cardboard Catherine Wheel (instructions below).

Play a game of rolling marbles down a chute (could be plastic rain guttering) and through a cardboard tube. Place a jar of marbles out of reach of the children and where the light from the window passes through it.

Have turns at looking through a kaleidoscope. Have you experimented with the kind that makes patterns out of objects around you, as well as the kind that has coloured pieces inside?

## TO CREATE

### A Catherine Wheel

Using thick, heavy cardboard cut out a circle about 10 cm (4") in diameter for each child. Cut out lots of circles of red, blue and yellow gummed paper, and cut them into thirds. The children can stick the gummed paper to both sides of the cardboard. Paint a thin border of white.

Now make two holes in each disk, one either side of centre. Pass a length of thin string through each hole and tie the ends to make a loop. Show the children how to hold the string loosely and wind the disk up tight. Then hold the string taut to make the disk spin and the colours mix and merge. If the disk keeps going off-centre, it is not heavy enough to balance properly; glue two together.

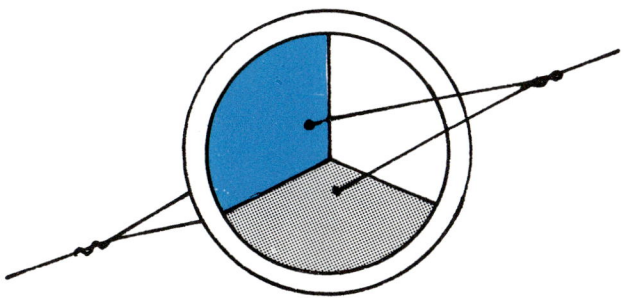

## Silver Swizzles

Give each child a 10 cm (4″) diameter circle of silver foil. Show them how to cut out a spiral, starting from the outer edge and working in. You will need some spare circles for attempts that go wrong, and good quality handicraft scissors (not pointed). With a darning needle, attach a loop of black thread to the inner edge of each spiral. A spiral in each hand to dance with leads the children into lovely twirling movements.

## Paper lanterns

Give each child a sheet of coloured paper. A4 (30 × 21 cm) is a good size. Show the children how to fold the paper in half lengthways. Crease well. About every 2 cm ($\frac{1}{2}$″), make a cut about 6 cm ($2\frac{1}{4}$″) deep, starting at the folded edge. Open out. Glue or staple the two ends together, overlapping. Use another 2 × 21 cm ($\frac{1}{2}$″ × 8″) strip for a handle, stapled across the top.

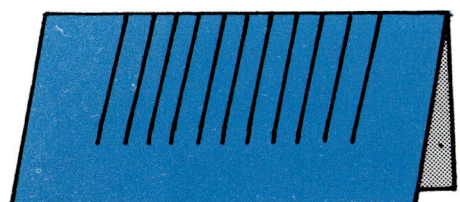

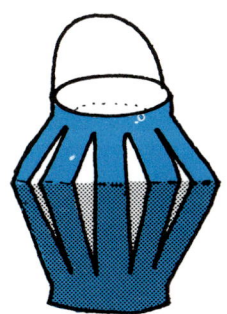

## TO FOLLOW UP

### Rose-tinted telescopes

Buy or save pieces of cellophane in several different colours. Sticky-tape pieces to the end of toilet roll tubes. Let the children interchange their 'telescopes' to see the world change colour. You may have to show them how to close the other eye when peering through one lens.

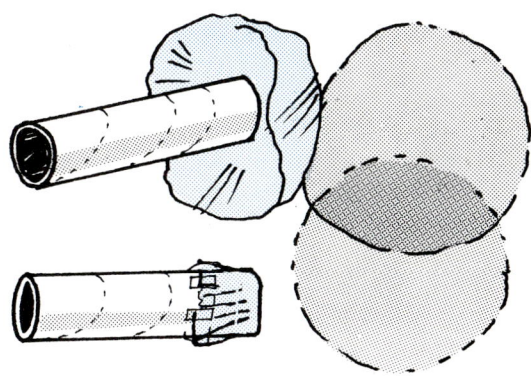

You can buy 'paddles' of different coloured transparent plastic material from educational suppliers. These are good for showing how the addition of a second colour changes the shade.

Some specialist paper shops and art shops sell coloured gelatine squares, which are used for coloured spotlight effects. These can be cut up and used for collages and colour experiments.

### Look at

THE ADVENTURES OF THE THREE COLOURS, by Annette Tison and Talus Taylor (Warne)
COLOURS, by James Gubb (Hamlyn)

## TO TALK ABOUT

### Halloween

On October 31, witches ride their broomsticks across the moon, so the superstition says. Their black cats hang on behind. It is a good excuse for a slightly spooky party. If you need artificial light in your hall or room, try covering the light shade with red cellophane for a deliciously sinister effect. If you have made a cobweb and some big, black spiders earlier in the month, they will help the Halloween atmosphere now. Can you and the children think of any other special effects that will scare mothers out of their wits at picking-up time? What about some black paper bats on black cotton thread fluttering above the doorway? And lots of little witches in black conical hats and cats in black masks instead of children to take home?

## TO LOOK FOR

### Wildlife

Hedgehogs, frogs, dormice, pet tortoises prepare to hibernate. Spiders spin. Wood pigeons still laying eggs; redwing and fieldfare birds arrive from further north to winter in Britain; starlings; barn owl; flocks of birds migrate south.

### Weather

Fine days, frosty nights. Check outdoor thermometer.

## TO JOIN IN

### Movement

*Halloween games*

Those children who like to join in games could try taking a bite out of apples on a string, with their hands behind their backs. Tie a piece of string across the room, or use an outdoor clothes line. Bind the apples round with string and dangle them from the line. One bite is difficult enough to manage. Their reward is the rest of the apple to eat.

Another game is passing an orange from one child to another without using hands. They must form a tight line, and pass it with their chins. Games for this age group should not be taken seriously.

### Action poem

*The Goblin*

A goblin lives in our house, in our house, in our house,
A goblin lives in our house all the year round.
  He bumps (gently bump the next child)
  And he jumps (jump)
  And he thumps (smack fist against open palm)
  And he stumps (stamp feet)
  He knocks (pretend to rap at door)
  And he rocks (rock on heels)
  And he rattles at the locks. (pretend to rattle door
                     with two hands)
A goblin lives in our house, in our house, in our house,
A goblin lives in our house, all the year round.

                         Rose Fyleman

### Story

MILLIONS OF CATS, by Wanda Gag.
(Notice that the illustrations are in black and white.)
  Look for a good reference picture of a bat at your library.

## TO INVESTIGATE

### A blot cat

Try to make a cat or a bat shape out of a big blob of thick black paint on white paper. Set out slim brushes for the children to move the paint about with. Try blowing a blot with a drinking straw to alter the outline. Try putting colour on damp blotting paper and watching it spread.

## TO CREATE

### A witch nose

Save paper pulp egg boxes. Some types have long, conical 'spacers'. Attach hat elastic to each side of a 'spacer' to make a witch's false nose.

**A witch's hat**

See August, week 4

**A witch's mask**

Bend a rectangle of black paper lengthways. Two semi-circles cut on the folded edge become circles for eye-holes when the paper is opened out. Thread or staple on hat elastic.

**A cat mask**

As above, with slanted eyes and ears.

**A pirate's eye patch and false teeth**

Cut an eye patch out of black paper or felt and attach hat elastic. Cut false teeth from orange peel (see January, week 2).

**TO FOLLOW UP**

**Marzipan treats for your Halloween party**

Ingredients:

100 g (¼ lb) ground almonds
200 g (½ lb) sieved icing sugar
¼ teaspoon almond essence
1 beaten egg

(Marzipan can also be bought ready for use.)

Method:

Add essence and icing sugar to almonds. Add egg a little at a time. Avoid making mixture too wet; it must not stick. If it does become sticky, add a little sieved flour. Knead. Divide the marzipan in sections and dye with a few drops of icing colourants. Let the children mould the marzipan into fruit and vegetable shapes, or whatever else occurs to them. Use cocoa to colour potato shapes; lemon icing colour for lemons, cochineal for apples, green icing colourant for leaves.

**Sweet baskets**

Save plastic mousse containers or yogurt pots. Staple on handles. Line with crumpled tissue paper. Place a few marzipan sweets inside a basket for each child.

**Cup puppets**

If you have used disposable cups for your party, wash and save them to make puppets.

1   Make a hole in the bottom big enough to push a pencil through.
2   Take a paper pulp cup from an egg box. Put some plasticine inside. Stick on features and cottonwool hair.
3   Paste pretty paper around the disposable cup. Bind two folded strips of paper with sticky tape, and stick them to the sides of the cup for arms.
4   Put a pencil through the cup. Push it into the plasticine inside the head.
5   Make your puppet 'talk', raising and lowering the head by moving the pencil up and down.

**Look at**

FLYING CREATURES, by Patricia Gray (Franklin Watts 'Wildlife' books)
SEA AND AIR MAMMALS, a Ladybird 'Animals of the World' book
BATS IN THE DARK, by John Kaufman (A. & C. Black)

# NOVEMBER week 1

## TO TALK ABOUT

### Guy Fawkes

November 5 is the anniversary of the Gunpowder Plot. On that day in 1605 a man named Guy Fawkes was caught trying to blow up the British Houses of Parliament with gunpowder. Every November 5 since then people have made 'Guys', effigies of Guy Fawkes, out of straw and paper to burn on top of a bonfire while fireworks are let off all around.

Fireworks are made with gunpowder and they are dangerous. Fireworks are waning in popularity because of the many accidental injuries to children they have caused. If any of the children in your group are going to a fireworks party, warn them not to pick up used sparklers—they are still hot enough to burn. Children should not hold any other type of firework in their hands. They must not investigate any firework that hasn't gone off, in case it blows up in their faces. Warn them not to stand next to the fireworks box in case a spark flies in, not to put fireworks in their pockets, and not to go too close to the fire. If all the rules are obeyed, everyone should be able to enjoy the spectacle without anyone getting hurt.

If you want to do something special for young children on Guy Fawkes night, a box of indoor fireworks can be interesting without being frightening. Indoor fireworks are relatively safe and inexpensive, but remember that you are still playing with fire, and must take care.

Popular Guy Fawkes fare is frankfurters with tomato sauce in bridge rolls, and potatoes baked in their jackets with butter inside.

## TO LOOK FOR

### Silver for the colour table

Moonshine is silver. Forks and spoons are often silver-plated. Sequins and glass beads and puddles that have turned to ice can be silvery. The sun shining on frost, snow or raindrops gives the world a silvery sparkle. Mirrors have silvered backs to help them reflect. Some coins are made of silver. The kitchen foil that you wrap around baking potatoes looks silvery. Grandmothers and grandfathers often have silver-coloured hair. Silver can be sparkling, or shiny,

or have a matt finish. If silver metal isn't polished regularly, it may become dull and eventually go black until it is polished again. Can anybody bring something silver that needs polishing to playgroup so that the children can see it become shiny again?

## TO JOIN IN

### Do the Hokey Pokey

There are many different versions of this folk dance. Here is one that most people seem to recognise.

The children form a large circle by holding hands, then letting hands drop to sides.

You put your right hand in,     (put right hand into circle)
You put your right hand out,     (put it out, towards back)
You put your right hand in and shake it all about.
You do the hokey pokey, (bend elbows, back of hands under chin, wag from side to side)
And you turn around, (twist right around)
That's what it's all about! (clap rhythm)
Oh, do the hokey pokey     (all hold hands and surge into centre of ring and back again)
Oh, do the hokey pokey (ditto)
Oh, do the hokey pokey (ditto)
That's what it's all about! (clap rhythm)

Repeat this with the left hand, then the right leg, left leg, head, and whole self.

### Rhyme

Here's to remember the fifth of November,
Gunpowder, treason and plot.
I see no reason why gunpowder treason,
Should ever be forgot!

### Poem

'Silver', by Walter de la Mare, from THE BOOK OF A THOUSAND POEMS.

### Story

Tell the November story from the Tufty road safety book from ROSPA House, which has a message about fireworks safety and wearing something white so as to be seen by cars at night. Illustrate the story with a felt board if you have one. (See 'Things for adults to make'.)

## TO INVESTIGATE

### Fireworks effects

Thick, light coloured paint looks luminescent against matt black paper. (Light coloured paint = a primary colour mixed with white.) It is an ideal medium for encouraging children to express their ideas of fireworks night.

## TO CREATE

### Glitter pictures

The children could make some Christmas cards in good time for December using glue and silver glitter. Show them how to fold a rectangle of paper double to form a square booklet. They can spread glue on the front cover and sprinkle silver glitter on from a plastic phial. If you place the cards on sheets of newspaper or on a tray, you will be able to re-use the surplus glitter that doesn't stick. Provide coloured as well as white paper and see if the children discover for themselves that glitter shows up best on a dark background.

## TO FOLLOW UP

### Making a Guy

Save laddered stockings or legs from old tights, and newspapers. Give each child three stockings. Put a pile of newspapers on the floor and show the children how to take a page at a time and scrunch it into a ball. Help each child to fill two stockings with paper. Tie a knot at both ends of each stocking. Take the third stocking. Tie the foot end around the middle of one stuffed stocking, which becomes the legs. Put some paper stuffing in the third stocking to fill out the body. Tie it around the other stuffed stocking, which becomes the arms. Stuff the top of the third

stocking with paper to make the head. Tie string around the top, leaving a loop with which to hang up Guy. Cover the floor with newspaper and the children can lay their Guys on the floor and paint them. Put a paper bag over the head of each Guy to give a better paint surface for the face. Hang them up to dry.

### A football

Fill the middle of a stocking with scrunched-up newspaper. Tie the two ends together and tuck out of the way. The children can kick it around for a football that won't do any damage.

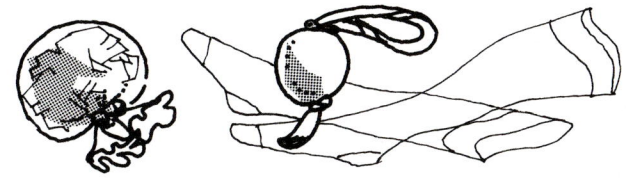

### A punch ball

Knot off the foot end of a stocking. Stuff the middle firmly to make a ball shape. Tie the other end into a loop, and hang it up for a swinging punch ball.

### A snowball fight

Make a line of tables either side of the room for the children to hide behind. Supply two piles of newspapers and let them make a pile of scrunched-up paper 'snowballs', to throw at each other. The tables could be pirate ships and the newspaper could become cannon balls. Finish off with a game of throwing the balls into a big bin to clear the floor.

# NOVEMBER week 2

## TO TALK ABOUT

### The Lord Mayor's Show

In November each year the newly-elected Lord Mayor of London leads a procession of aldermen through the City to the Mansion House, where the Queen confirms his appointment. The mayor travels in a horse-drawn coach. The wealth, splendour, industry and endeavour of the City are represented in a parade of decorated floats. The effigies of two giants are always in the procession, Gog and Magog. Legend says that they defended old London town many centuries ago.

Watch for film of the Lord Mayor's Show being shown on children's television programmes. Show the children any pictures of the parade in newspapers or magazines.

Another kind of show that visits big towns in November is the circus.

## TO LOOK FOR

### Fruit in the shops now

Apples, oranges, pears, tangerines

## TO JOIN IN

### Movement

*Giants and fairies*

Shake a tambourine or play treble notes on a piano as the children dance like fairies, quickly, softly, lightly. Strike the tambourine hard or play bass notes on the piano. The fairies run away and the children pretend to be giants, lumbering about in a slow, loud, heavy dance.

*Monkeys and elephants*

The children could pretend to be monkeys in a circus, scampering about, doing tricks. Then they could try being elephants, the giants of the animal kingdom, moving slowly and majestically on all fours. What do the children think an elephant's skin feels like? What does a monkey's coat feel like?

*Circus giants*

Is anybody going to the circus this month? There might be a giant there—a man walking on stilts that are covered by trousers to look like very long legs.

### Rhymes

There was an old person of Wilts,
Who constantly walked upon stilts.
He wreathed them with lilies
And daffy-down-dillies,
That elegant person of Wilts.

Edward Lear

See Saw Sacredown,
Which is the way to London town?
One foot up and one foot down,
That is the way to London town.

Hey diddle dinkety poppety pet,
The merchants of London they wear scarlet;
Silk in the collar and gold in the hem,
So merrily march the merchant men.

### Poem

'The Blind Men and the Elephant', by John Godfrey Saxe (THE BOOK OF A THOUSAND POEMS)

### Nursery stories

'Jack and the Beanstalk'
'Dick Whittington'

## TO INVESTIGATE

### A feel bag

Keep a draw-string bag full of scraps of cloth for the children to sort through whenever they feel like it. Scraps can be used for collage, for dolls clothes and blankets, or glued to a piece of old sheet to make a patchwork. Tell the children the names of all the different types of material. Then have a game where the children close their eyes, select a scrap, and try to tell by the feel what it is. Make a sorting game of placing scraps in order of softness, or thickness, or smoothness. Point out basic patterns like checks, tartans, florals, tweed, stripes, spots, paisley.

**A feel board** (for you to make for the children)

Select a piece of board to suit your purpose. It could be a small piece of hardboard that is easy to store and light for the children to handle, or a long strip of board that can be mounted permanently at child height on the wall. Glue on as many different textures as you can. Some examples are pot scouring cloths, hessian, tweed, carpet, fur, velvet, satin, net, brocade, ruffles, smocking, blanket, towelling, feathers, suede, tree bark, loofah, sponge, pumice stone. Be ready to talk about the different textures when you see the children experimenting.

## TO CREATE

### A cloth montage

Let the children cut up and stick on scraps of many types of cloth, silver and gold paper, etc., to make any kind of picture they like. They might like to take the colour and richness of the Lord Mayor's Show as their inspiration, although the results may turn out to be completely different. Provide wood spills, which can be broken up to make outlines of a coach, house, road, and washed and flattened milk bottle tops, which make good wheels. Cut out pictures of horses, soldiers, and cheering crowd from magazines.

## TO FOLLOW UP

### Tin can stilts

Save identical empty tin cans, two for each child. Small size pet food tins are ideal. Wash well. Make sure the rim of the opened end is not sharp. With a large nail or bradawl, punch a hole either side of each tin, just below the rim of the unopened end. Smooth back any jagged edges as much as possible. Measure the distance from a child's feet to hands at sides.

You will need a little over twice this length of strong string for each tin. Thread it through the holes and tie to make a loop. The child stands on the tins, lifting up a foot at a time with the string. With practice, four-year-olds can manage this quite well.

### Circus lions

If you have a games hoop, you can play 'circus'. The children pretend to be lions, stalking on all fours around the circus ring, and jumping through the hoop you hold up. They could each have a lion-sounding name, which could be printed on paper and safety-pinned on them. Each has to obey your commands when you call its name, though not without a bit of aggressive 'acting up', rolling over, snapping and growling. Watch that this doesn't really frighten some of the timid tiny tots. Follow it with a quiet activity. Look at pictures of different kinds of 'big cats'.

### Look at

THE CIRCUS, by Brian Wildsmith (Oxford University Press)
CIRCUS, by Dick Bruna (Methuen)

# NOVEMBER week 3

## TO TALK ABOUT

### Wishes and charms

Now is the time to mix rich plum puddings and cakes that will mature by Christmas. It was once traditional to throw silver charms into the pudding mix, and it was considered very lucky to find one of these charms in your slice of pudding. No doubt it was very unlucky if you swallowed it! Small silver coins were sometimes used instead of charms. If you can afford to, add a few to your mixture. Boil the coins first for the sake of hygiene.

Everyone who stirs the plum pudding is entitled to a wish. Whoever makes the first cut in a Christmas or birthday cake may make a wish, but must not tell it. Everyone is allowed a wish before biting into a mince pie, which is meant to remind us of the manger with baby Jesus cradled inside.

If you are making a plum pudding and giving everyone a chance to stir, set out the ingredients for the children to sniff. The smells of rich food, spices and cooking are especially welcome during winter months when there are no sweet-smelling flowers to give our noses a treat.

## TO LOOK FOR

### Plant life

Japonica. Ivy. Holly berries and mistletoe begin to ripen. Farmers plough fields and begin hedging and ditching. Mushroom umbrellas spring up. Look for 'fairy rings' of toadstools growing outwards from a central root. Fungus, lichens, moss. Fallen leaves make a quilt of leaf mould for the soil. Puddles turn into sheets of silver ice.

## TO JOIN IN

### Poems

*Pudding Charms*

Our Christmas pudding was made in November,
All they put in it, I quite well remember:
Currants and raisins, and sugar and spice,
Orange peel, lemon peel—everything nice
Mixed up together, and put in a pan.

'When you've stirred it,' said Mother, 'as much as
   you can,
We'll cover it over, that nothing may spoil it,
And then in the copper, tomorrow we'll boil it.'

That night, when we children were all fast asleep,
A real fairy godmother came crip-a-creep!
She wore a red cloak, and a tall steeple hat
(Though nobody saw her but Tinker, the cat!)
And out of her pocket a thimble she drew,
A button of silver, a silver horse-shoe,
And, whisp'ring a charm, in the pudding pan popped
   them,
Then flew up the chimney directly she dropped them;
And even old Tinker pretended he slept
(With Tinker a secret is sure to be kept!),
So nobody knew, until Christmas came round,
And there, in the pudding, these treasures we found.

                Charlotte Druitt Cole

*Mincemeat*

Sing a song of mincemeat,
Currants, raisins, spice,
Apples, sugar, nutmeg,
Everything that's nice,
Stir it with a ladle,
Wish a lovely wish,
Drop it in the middle
Of your well-filled dish,
Stir again for good luck,
Pack it all away
Tied in little jars and pots,
Until Christmas Day.

              Elizabeth Gould

## TO INVESTIGATE

### A smell table

What can you smell out of doors this month? There are berries and green leaves, but they do not have much smell. Some of the fungus and puff ball mushrooms give out a musty smell if you break them with your shoe.

What can you smell indoors this month? Have a table full of pleasant smells—pot pourri from summer gardens; perfume dregs; nutmeg, cloves and spice in spill-proof containers or sprinkled sparingly on saucers; vapour rub; coffee beans; anything else you can think of that has a distinctive smell.

Have a guessing game. Blindfold an adult helper and ask the children to pass things for the helper to recognise by smell. See if one of the children can pass the blindfold test. Give all the volunteers a try.

Try another guessing game. You think of a simple object, say the table in your room. Give the children clues such as 'It has four legs'. Keep adding to the information and answering questions until someone guesses the object correctly. Try it with something a little bit more difficult or something funny. Does it have a smell? All have a sniff around the room and try to say what sort of smell different things have.

## Superstitions

Here are some strange ideas to think about. The rhyme about the pin seems to have some sense to it.

See a pin and pick it up
All the day you'll have good luck.
See a pin and let it lay,
You'll have bad luck all the day.

If you sneeze on Monday, you sneeze for danger;
Sneeze on Tuesday, kiss a stranger;
Sneeze on Wednesday, sneeze for a letter;
Sneeze on Thursday, something better;
Sneeze on Friday, sneeze for sorrow;
Sneeze on Saturday, joy for tomorrow.

If you remember to say 'white rabbits' three times before you say any other word on the first day of the month, you will get a present in that month.

If you drink tea and find tea leaves at the bottom of the cup, choose the largest. It is your 'stranger'. Is he or she long and lean or short and stout? Place him on top of your left fist. Bring your right fist down on top of him as you recite the days of the week. The day on which he sticks to the top fist is the day on which he will visit you.

## TO CREATE

### Paper flowers

Search outdoors for suitable fallen twigs to make flower stems for a vase, and larger branched twigs to make indoor flowering trees. Larger twigs can be set in a family size yogurt pot filled with plaster of paris. Stemmed flowers can be arranged with bracken fronds in the fancier types of yogurt containers, tall and thin or goblet shaped. Remove the print first with wire wool. Paint them gold if you like.

Flowers can be made of tissues, tissue paper or crêpe paper. Probably the simplest and least frustrating flowers for under-fives to make are saucer-size circles of coloured tissue paper, gathered in the middle. They can be attached to a stem with sticky tape. Paper flowers look almost as pretty as the real ones we see in summer. But they don't have any smell! Make a snowy tree by putting a little glue on cottonwool balls, dipping them in glitter, and then gluing them on the large twig you have brought indoors.

## TO FOLLOW UP

### A birds' pudding

Ask the children to save and bring to playgroup pieces of bacon rind, scraps of cooked meat, cheese, broken biscuits, pet food nuts and grain, stale bread, apple cores and anything else they can think of that birds might like to eat. Mince it all up or dice the larger pieces. Mix well. Grease a bowl and fill it with the mixture. Melt some lard and pour it over the mixture. Put in a piece of string to hang the pudding up by. Leave it to set hard, then hang it from a tree for the birds.

# NOVEMBER week 4

## TO TALK ABOUT

### Where does Father Christmas live?

Christmas time is nearly here. Where do the children think Father Christmas lives? Most seem to think he lives somewhere where there is lots of ice and snow . . . somewhere near the North Pole, somewhere where reindeer live.

Some creatures that look rather like little men live near the South Pole, in the Antarctic Ocean. They are penguins. These birds don't fly, they swim. When they come ashore they waddle along very awkwardly, and often march in line like soldiers. They nest on the rocky Antarctic coast in October, and lay their eggs in November. Lots of baby penguins hatch at Christmas. King and Emperor penguins do not build nests, but carry their one large egg about with them, between their feet. See what you and the children can find out about penguins.

## TO LOOK FOR

### Wildlife

Fox cubs born in the spring are now big enough to hunt food for themselves, and some people hunt the foxes. It is springtime in the Antarctic. Penguins begin laying eggs.

### Weather

Fog, rain, frost, possible mild spells. The sky is pink and purple at sunset. Stars seem to come out early and are easily seen. Check your thermometer. Has the mercury dropped as low as 5°C yet?

## TO JOIN IN

### Movement

*Marching penguins*

Show the children how to make 'penguin feet'. Draw a shape on cardboard for each foot, like a snowshoe with three webbed toes. Help the children to cut them out. Attach to feet with large rubber bands. Now all shuffle along stiffly like penguins, one behind the other, flapping wings at sides. See if the children can do it with a ball as a make-believe egg between their feet. (One little boy was so captivated by this idea

that he insisted on *becoming* a penguin, with cardboard wings, a white front and a mask with a beak. He was so eager that he spontaneously measured his head with a piece of elastic and cut it to the right size for his mask.)

Have a penguin egg race, trying not to lose the ball from between the feet, or a kangaroo race, taking little hopping jumps with the ball held between the knees.

### Riddle

A house full, a hole full,
You cannot catch a bowlful.
What is it?
Answer: Mist.

### Songs

A-hunting we will go,
A-hunting we will go,
We'll catch a little fox and put him in a box,
And then we'll let him go.

(Music in THIS LITTLE PUFFIN)

'A fox set out on a chilly night', on record CHILDREN'S FAVOURITES (MFP 1175), and in book form, illustrated by Peter Spier (World's Work).

### Poems

*November*

November is a spinner
Spinning in the mist,
Weaving such a lovely web
of gold and amethyst.
In among the shadows
She spins till close of day,
Then quietly she folds her hands
And puts her work away.

Margaret Rose

Put your finger in Foxie's hole    (place index and
    middle finger of right hand across index and middle
    finger of left hand with a gap for Foxie's hole)
Foxie's not at home.
Foxie's at the back door,  (when child puts finger in
    hole, gently nip it between thumb and ring finger,

kept out of sight underneath hole)
Picking a marrow bone.

'The Three Foxes', by A. A. Milne (OXFORD BOOK OF CHILDREN'S VERSE)

**Story book**

TOPSY AND TIM'S FOGGY DAY, by Jean and Gareth Adamson (Blackie)

## TO INVESTIGATE

### Where do they live?

Reindeer live in cold lands. Penguins live in cold seas. Where do giraffes live? And emus? Use toy animals or cut out pictures of animals to make a game of guessing which ones live in a cold climate and which live in a hot climate. You could make a hot/cold chart or scrapbook with pictures cut from magazines.

## TO CREATE

### Puppets

*A penguin*

Save toilet roll tubes. Anchor each to the table with a wodge of plasticine. The children can now paint the tubes three-quarters black, one quarter white lengthways, turning the plasticine so they can paint right around. While the paint is drying, show children how to roll one white paper tissue into a ball, and wrap another tissue around it. When the paint is dry, push the ends of the tissue into the cardboard tube so that the ball becomes a head. For each penguin cut 2 eyes, 1 beak, 2 wings, and a base that looks like two webbed feet, out of black paper. The children can glue on eyes and beak. Sticky-tape wings and feet.

*A Christmas angel*

Save toilet roll tubes. Buy white, silver or gold paper doilies. Make a paper tissue head, as for the penguins. Cut a dainty mouth and two eyes out of coloured gummed paper and stick on. Fold paper doilies in half to find the centre. Cut down a little way from the centre to make an opening. Fold in half the other way. Cut down a little. The children can put these over the tubes for angel dresses. Bend pipe cleaners around for arms. Use a few strands of wool laid across sticky tape for hair. Half a paper doily, pleated slightly and attached to the back with sticky tape, becomes wings.

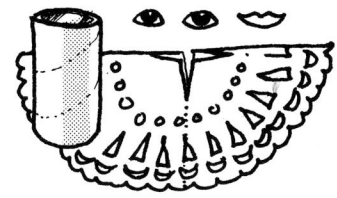 

*A reindeer*

Save toilet roll tubes. Push in a paper tissue head. Roll a length of sticky tape, bend and shape it to make antlers. Tape antlers in position on head. Wrap pipe cleaners around at front and back to make legs, or make holes and stick in wood spills cut to the right length.

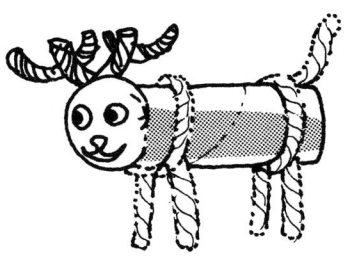

*Father Christmas* (a hand puppet)

In advance, cut out a 'head and two arms' shape to fit a child's hand. Cut two shapes in red crêpe paper for each child. Also cut one large circle and two small circles in pink tissue paper for each child. Supply good glue, cottonwool, gummed paper, black sticky tape or passé partout.

1 The child glues the two pieces of red crêpe together around the edges.
2 Glue on pink circles for face and hands.
3 Stick on features.
4 Glue on cottonwool trim around face, moustache and whiskers, and trim down front of red coat.
5 Stick black belt around middle.

## TO FOLLOW UP

Have a free play acting-out session with the puppets.

**Look at**

PENGUINS, by Louis Darling (Angus & Robertson)

# DECEMBER   week 1

## TO TALK ABOUT

### Advent

Advent is the name given to the period leading up to Christmas. Advent calendars usually cover twenty-five days from December 1 to Christmas Day, and they have a Christmasy picture for each day to remind us of the coming event.

Ask the children to bring yogurt pots or empty matchboxes to playgroup if their mothers have any to spare. You can use them to make a different kind of advent calendar, full of surprises.

## TO LOOK FOR

### White for the colour table

White is the colour of snow. When snow falls at Christmas time it seems extra exciting. The world outside is hushed and bright and pure. Inside, our homes are cosy and cheerful. White is the colour of light, of candles, and of icing sugar for Christmas cakes. Father Christmas's beard is white. Sheets and pillowcases are often white. If you mix white paint with coloured paint, you make a lighter shade.

## TO JOIN IN

### Advent surprises

You will need 25 matchboxes or 25 yogurt pots. Write the name of a Christmas carol, a poem or a story on paper and put one inside each pot or box. Select five basic carols, etc., so that each is repeated at random five times until December 25, and the

children really start to know them. If you have saved 25 matchboxes, glue them together to form a chest of drawers. If you have saved yogurt pots, cut out circles of greaseproof paper a little larger than the top, cover and secure with rubber bands. Paint the pots or cover them with coloured paper to make them more attractive. Stack the pots in a triangular Christmas tree shape. Each day a different child can break the seal or open a matchbox drawer to discover what the day's surprise is going to be.

### Song suggestions

'Away in a manger' and 'Jingle Bells' (THE PUFFIN SONG BOOK).
'I saw three ships come sailing in on Christmas Day in the morning' and 'Dame get up and bake your pies' (OXFORD NURSERY SONG BOOK).
'Rudolph the red-nosed reindeer' (sheet music or on record).

### Poem suggestions

Little Jack Horner
Sat in a corner,
Eating his Christmas pie.
He put in his thumb,
And pulled out a plum,
And said 'What a good boy am I'.

Christmas is coming
And the ducks are getting fat.
Please put a penny in the old man's hat.
If you haven't got a penny, then a ha'penny will do.
If you haven't got a ha'penny, then
God bless you!

### For you to read to the children:

''Twas the night before Christmas', by Clement C. Moore.

Three poems from THE BOOK OF A THOUSAND POEMS: 'Santa Claus' ('He comes in the night! He comes in the night!')
'A Child's Christmas Carol' ('There was a little baby once'), by Christine Chaundler
'Song' ('Why do the bells of Christmas ring?'),by Eugene Field

**Stories**

'The Christmas Story', as told on Play School, BBC
Publications

CHRISTMAS IN THE STABLE, Brockhampton Press
HOW SANTA CLAUS HAD A LONG AND DIFFICULT
JOURNEY DELIVERING HIS PRESENTS, Longman
Young Books

## TO INVESTIGATE

### The effects of white

This week mix powder paint colours thick and strong.
Also mix plenty of pure white. Let the children
experiment with mixing the paint on paper.

Even daytime can be fairly dark in December. Tie
a piece of old white sheet on each child's arm. Turn
off artificial light. See how the white shows up in the
dimness more clearly than dark colours. Switch on
a torch and see how the white shows up even more
in its beam. Suggest that children try to wear something white on their way to and from playgroup on
dark and foggy days so that they can be seen clearly
by passing cars. School children should wear something white, or reflecting road safety arm bands,
especially if they wear dark uniforms.

### Torch games

Cut a small flying bat shape out of black card. See
what happens when you place it against the torch
glass. What happens when you hold it further away
in the beam? Cut a child's initial letter out of a circle
of black card and shine the torch through it. Hold
coloured tissue paper across the torch glass to make
coloured light.

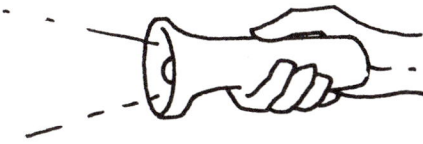

## TO CREATE

### A white angel

This is the simplest kind of Christmas angel. Take a
toilet roll tube. The child can draw a face on the top
third with felt-tip pens. Glue on cottonwool hair.

Attach a long white crêpe paper skirt and wings with
sticky tape. Dab with glue and sprinkle with silver
glitter.

## TO FOLLOW UP

### A Nativity scene

For under-fives, felt figures that they can move
around on a felt board may be more satisfying than
three-dimensional models. You will find instructions
for making a felt board in 'Things for adults to make'.

### Paper chains

You can buy paper ready cut, or cut coloured
gummed paper into strips. First show the children
how to make the paper strip into a ring. Then show
them how to loop another paper strip through the
ring before sticking it closed. Children enjoy this
repetitive activity, which takes a certain amount of
skill. As with bead threading, I have seen children
thoroughly enjoying random colour selection, whose
enthusiasm faded when an adult interfered in a well-
meaning attempt to teach colour sense. Tread
carefully!

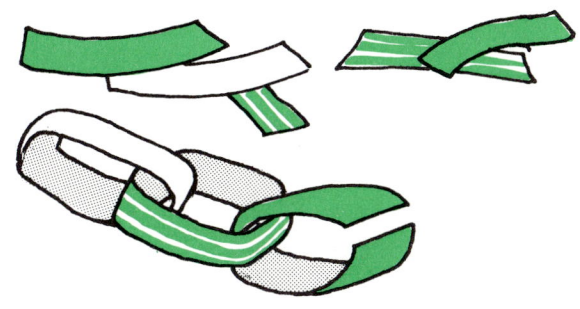

### Snowflake Christmas cards

Paper-tearing makes patterns as individual as snowflake crystals. Give the children each a square of
white paper. Show them how to fold it in half
diagonally, then in half again. Tear tiny pieces out
of each edge, then unfold to show a pattern of holes.
Paste on a coloured paper background.

Make a different pattern, beginning with a round
shape. Make larger holes. Use more intricate folds.

# DECEMBER week 2

## TO TALK ABOUT

### Sacks

Father Christmas carries a sack of toys. Can the children think of anyone else who carries a sack? The coal man does. The postman does. Postmen have very heavy sacks at this time of year, delivering Christmas cards full of good wishes that families and friends send to one another.

Have the children received any greeting cards at home yet? Have they made cards to give to their own families? A lot of envelopes and stamps are used at Christmas. Most of them are thrown away once the card inside has reached its destination. Some charities make money from used stamps. You might like to inquire if they would be useful to a local organisation. If parents saved the stamps for the children to bring to playgroup, you might collect quite a lot over the Christmas period towards a good cause. The children will find it exciting to watch the pile grow through their own efforts, and they are not too young to appreciate that Christmas is a time for thinking of others.

Write to the post office head office; they sometimes have wall charts with simple illustrations explaining what the postman does, which they will send to you.

## TO LOOK FOR

### Fruit in the shops now

Honeydew melons, apples, oranges, pears, tangerines, nuts. (Try some roasted chestnuts.)

## TO JOIN IN

### A sack race

The children climb into onion sacks, old pillowslips or large paper carrier bags. They jump along, holding the sack with both hands. Watch for the smaller ones losing their balance. If you have to use a polished or concrete floor indoors, save your sack race for summer and hold it on grass outdoors.

### A letter hunt

There are two kinds of letters—letters you post and letters of the alphabet. This is a hunt for letters of the alphabet. Divide the children into teams of about five, and give each team a letter, a, b, c, etc. Each team has a paper supermarket carrier bag (not plastic, which can smother) with the appropriate letter printed large on it. On the wall, mount a chart showing the things that each team has to help collect and put in the carrier bag. Draw each object, which should be simple in shape and spelling. Print the name, and tell the children what it is. For example, 'a' team could hunt for a (toy) animal, aeroplane, apple, acorn, and apron; 'b' team could hunt for a book, block, ball, bead, button; 'c' team could hunt for a crayon, Christmas card, cup, coin, car. As each team brings back its quota of objects, write 1st, 2nd and 3rd at the bottom of each list on the wall.

### Action Poem

*The Postman*

Here comes the postman,
With a full sack
Of Christmas cards
And letters on his back.

He's walking up our path now,
At the door he knocks,
And he puts lots of Christmas cards
Through our letter box.
I.C.

*The Postman*

Rat-a-tat-tat, Rat-a-tat-tat,
Rat-a-tat-tat tattoo!
That's the way the postman goes,
Rat-a-tat-tat tattoo!
Every morning at half-past eight
You hear a bang at the garden gate,
And Rat-a-tat-tat, Rat-a-tat-tat,
Rat-a-tat-tat tattoo!
Clive Sansom

### Song

*Sing the alphabet*

abcdefg
hijklmnop
qrs & tuv
w & xyz!

'A was an Apple Pie', in THE PUFFIN BOOK OF NURSERY RHYMES

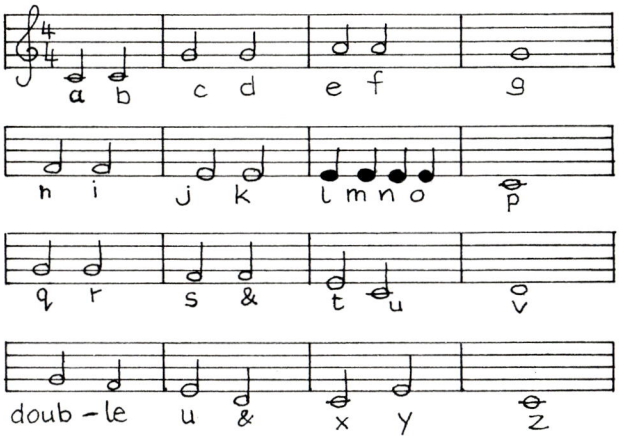

## TO INVESTIGATE

### A letters table

Take the objects that the children have collected and set them out on a table in groups labelled a, b, c.

Sound the letters phonetically. Explain that some letters have more than one sound. Ask the children to look around the room and see what other things they can see that begin with a, b or c. Suitable objects can be placed in the appropriate groups on the table, which could have a ring drawn around them to show that each is a separate set of things. Have a simple phonetic game of 'I spy', confined to the objects on the table.

## TO CREATE

### Funny alphabets

Give each child a piece of paper and pencil or felt-tip pen, and see what sort of funny things he can make out of the letters a, b and c. For instance, a could become an ant, b could become a butterfly, and c could become a caterpillar, but it could be anything, not necessarily something that begins with the sound of the letter.

## TO FOLLOW UP

If the children have enjoyed playing some of the alphabet games, have a hunt for the next three letters of the alphabet the following day, and so on.

### Alphabet and number games

As Christmas presents for the children make alphabet and number sorting games. Divide the alphabet in two, and rule two pieces of thick cardboard so there is a square for each letter. Do the same with the numbers 1 to 20, so that 1 to 10 is on one card, and 11 to 20 on the other. These are the base cards. Now, on thinner card, rule squares the same size for each letter and number. You can print the letters and numbers with a felt-tip pen, use numbers from calendars and letters from magazines, or use transfer letters, such as Letraset.

Cut out these squares and mix them up. The children then cover the base cards with the matching cut-out squares. The children can play alone or in small groups.

| a | b | c | d | e |
|---|---|---|---|---|
| f | g | h | i | j |
| k | l | m | | |

| n | o | p | q | r |
|---|---|---|---|---|
| s | t | u | v | w |
| x | y | z | | |

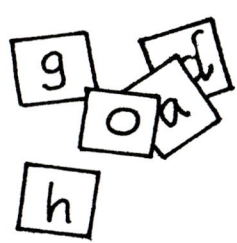

# DECEMBER week 3

## TO TALK ABOUT

### Paper shapes

Paper can be folded into useful shapes—a fan or paper hat, for example. Paper can be folded to give us a surprise. Here is one way to make a paper fold surprise. It isn't a very nice surprise, but children love it.

1  Take a strip of paper about 5 cm (2″) wide and 20 cm (8″) long. Fold it in half (10 cm). Fold it in half again.

2  Open back one flap, keeping the remaining three-quarters of the strip concertina-folded.

3  Draw a face taking up the whole of the top square. The mouth finishes below the folded line and is continued on the bottom square. The bottom square becomes a jacket, with buttons down the front. Colour both squares.

4  Open up the folded centre squares, and draw a large tongue. Colour it red.

5  Show the children your portrait with the centre fold hidden. Then pull the strip straight to show the tongue sticking out at them. They will all want to make one to take home to surprise their parents.

## TO LOOK FOR

### Plant life

Christmas rose, holly berries, mistletoe, ivy, laurel leaves

## TO JOIN IN

### Movement

*Living shapes*

What sort of shapes can the children fold themselves into? Bend at the waist and let arms hang at right angles towards the floor. That makes a square kind of shape. Bend the knees a little and touch the floor with hands. That looks more like a triangle. Crouch on the floor and bend at all the 'folds'—knees, hips, waist, elbows—tuck head well in. That makes a circle shape. Now have the children stand up and make a big circle with their arms, fingers interlocking. See if they can thread their whole bodies through their arms, starting with the feet. It can be done. What other shapes can the children make by themselves or with a partner?

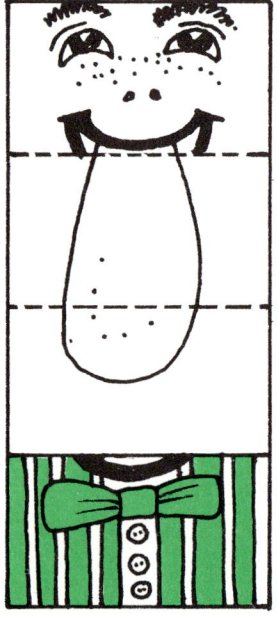

## TO CREATE

### A paper-fold house

Each child begins with a square of gummed paper.

1 Show the children how to make a cut a little way in from the top right hand corner. This is going to be the chimney.

2 Fold the paper in half. Cut to a point to make a sloping roof, leaving the chimney intact. Cut half a door at the bottom of the centre fold.

3 Fold in half again. Cut half a window on the folded edge opposite the door.

4 Now unfold and you have a house. The folds will help it to stand up by itself. The children can stick the house on a square of gummed paper in a contrasting colour. Other squares can be cut up to make curtains, people and animals in a fanciful picture.

Show the children how a flat sheet of paper will not stand on edge. Then fold the paper in half or in concertina folds so that it will stand up. Experiment with other paper-fold ways of making figures stand.

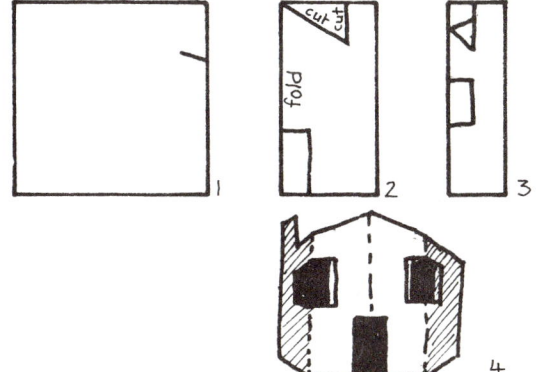

## TO INVESTIGATE

### Christmas mobiles

The simplest mobiles are made by tying light objects to a wire coat hanger with black thread. Hang the coat hanger at a safe distance above a radiator so that the current of warm air keeps the objects moving. Glass Christmas tree balls and silver swizzels (October, week 3) make pretty mobiles.

Another idea with which children can help is a picture mobile. The children can sort through old Christmas cards and magazines to find Christmas scenes that appeal to them. Provide each group with similar-sized round pastry cutters. The children can trace a circle around each picture chosen, and cut it out. Line up 16 circles, pictures face-down on the table. Draw an arrow on the back of each to show which way is 'up'. Brush on glue. Cut four long lengths of black thread. Place each length of thread across the backs of four circles. Brush glue onto the backs of another 16 circles. Place these over the cotton, back to back with the first circles. Smooth down. When dry, tie the top of the lengths of cotton, suitably spaced, along a wire coat hanger.

## TO FOLLOW UP

### A manger scene

Tell a simple version of the Christmas story. If the children would like to make a picture of it, they could use the paper-fold technique for cutting out a stable, adding the crib, Mary, Joseph and some animals as they like.

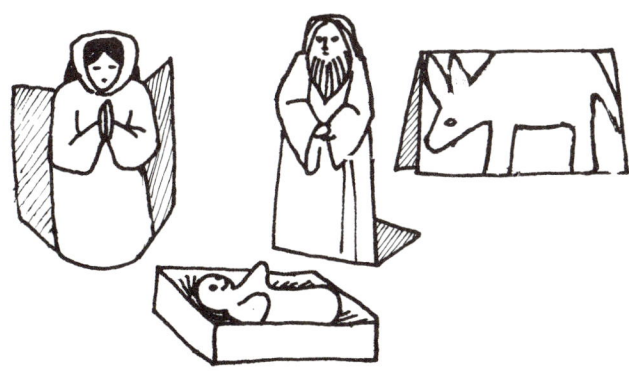

# DECEMBER week 4

## TO TALK ABOUT

### Tails

The star that shone on the stable at Bethlehem must have been very large and bright. Sometimes stars have tails of light. Then they are called comets. Many living creatures have a tail of some kind. Tails are useful things. Birds have tails to help them move through the air. Fish have tails to help them move through the water. Kangaroos have tails to help them move across the ground. Monkeys swing by their tails. Squirrels wrap their tails around themselves to keep warm. Cows use their tails to swish off flies. Elephants have big bodies, but small tails; their long trunks can keep flies off the front half of their bodies. Which creatures that we might see this month have tails, and how do they use them?

## TO LOOK FOR

### Wildlife

Robin, wren, peewit (lapwing), heron, mallard duck; bats are in their winter sleep; stoats are on the prowl in their white winter coats.

### Weather

Cold, misty, possible snow.

## TO JOIN IN

### Movement

*Catch the tail*

All the children line up behind the leader, arms around the waist of the person in front, making a long tail. The leader has to try to catch the last person in the line, swinging first one way and then the other as the tail tries to escape without breaking the line.

### Three Poems from THE BOOK OF A THOUSAND POEMS

'A tragic story' (the tale of a pigtail), by W. M. Thackeray

'The Three Little Pigs' (Umph! Umph! Umph!), by Sir Alfred A. Scott-Gatty

*The Elephant*

When people call this beast to mind,
They marvel more and more
At such a little tail behind
So LARGE a trunk before.
Hilaire Belloc

### Poem

*A Cow*

Four stiff standers, (legs)
Four dolly-danders, (udder)
Two lookers, (eyes)
Two crookers, (horns)
And a wig-wag. (tail)

### Story books

PIG TALE, by Helen Oxenbury
BANDICOOT AND HIS FRIENDS, by Violet Philpott (Dent)

## TO INVESTIGATE

### Hair sets

Do any of the children in your group have pigtails? How many? Draw a circle on a large piece of paper and draw in as many heads as have pigtails. How many children have straight hair? Add another circle to your chart and draw in the number who have straight hair. How many have curly hair? Draw the appropriate number of curly heads inside another circle. Can the children recognise themselves in the circles?

## TO CREATE

### Tails and tales

Let the children make clay or plasticine animals that have interesting tails. Talk about them.

### Christmas crackers

Save toilet roll tubes. Buy red crêpe paper. Cut the pack in half with strong scissors. Cut off suitable lengths for the children to wrap around the tubes. Keep in place with a piece of sticky tape at the middle. Wrap sticky tape tightly around one end. Slip in a few small animal cracker biscuits or jelly sweets in the shape of snakes, fish and animals, wrapped in cellophane. Now wrap sticky tape tightly around the other end to make a cracker shape. To make the crackers more attractive, trim the pleated ends with pinking shears, and tie them with gold crocheting yarn. Cut flower pictures out of seed catalogues and paste on the join.

A ball of gold crocheting yarn ties up a heap of presents and can be crocheted into gold chains for bracelets and pendants.

### A paper Christmas tree

For this you will need a large sheet of strong paper. Place it on the floor and draw an outline of a Christmas tree in a pot. Provide plenty of tissue paper, green for the tree, brown for the trunk, red for the pot. Provide a shallow trough of wallpaper paste. The children can scrunch up the tissue paper, dip it in the paste, and position it inside the drawn outline. Next day, when the glue has dried, Christmas tree decorations can be stuck on with sticky tape. Fix the tree to the wall with display putty.

### Matchbox baby

Push the drawers out of empty small matchboxes. Supply the children with pre-cut gummed paper shapes. Each child can stick various shapes together inside the matchbox drawer to make a doll. Replace the drawer in the matchbox, and each child has a secret baby to keep in a pocket. Alternatively, an adult could cut 'rockers' out of the matchbox sleeve, and glue them to the drawer ends to make a cradle.

## TO FOLLOW UP

### How sharp are your ears?

Are all the children going to listen for Father Christmas on Christmas Eve? Here are some listening exercises to make sure their ears are sharp enough.

The children sit in a semi-circle around the group leader. They close their eyes tight while she chooses something that makes a distinctive sound. Then they try to guess what it is, without peeping. Some sounds you could try are a baby's rattle; scissors being opened and closed; milk being poured into cups; humming on tissue paper against a comb; using a staple machine; flicking through the pages of a book; footsteps. Give clues if the children cannot guess right away.

Now try moving about the room. See if the children can point in the direction your voice is coming from, keeping their eyes closed.

### Farmyard

Give each child the name of a different kind of animal that makes a distinctive sound. Tell a story, introducing the names of all the animals. As each animal is mentioned, the child who has been given that animal's name has to make its sound. Whenever you say 'farmyard', all the children have to make animal noises at once.

### Look at

DO YOU KNOW ABOUT TAILS?, by Kathleen A. Shoesmith (Burke)
STRAIGHT HAIR, CURLY HAIR, by Augusta Goldin (A. & C. Black)

# Things for adults to make for children

## A JACK-IN-A-BOX

You will need:

1 hair roller
1 table tennis ball
felt scraps
plaster of paris and cardboard
*or* a thick piece of foam rubber
1 small, heavy duty cardboard box with a strong lid
*or* a plastic carton with a lid, such as those in which cottage cheese is packaged
tough tape
glue
narrow cord
1 brass paper clip
needle and button thread

1 Remove the inner brush from hair roller. Leave the outer webbing on the spring, but ease off one end, and stretch spring to make it longer.
2 Pierce 2 holes in table tennis ball and sew it to webbing end of spring.
3 Cut out jacket with sleeves from felt. Cut out hands in white felt and glue in place. Make bow-tie in contrasting colour. Glue to spring.

4 Paint eyes and mouth on ball. Glue on a button nose. Glue on wool hair.
5 Twist the bare end of the spring through a thick pad of foam rubber that has to be squashed a bit to fit into the box, and glue the pad in place;

*or* set some plaster of paris smoothly in the bottom of the box or carton, cut a piece of cardboard to fit on top of the plaster, make a hole in the cardboard off-centre and twist the spring through it, and glue the cardboard firmly to the plaster base so that the spring is held upright.
6 If you have used a carton, glue a cord tab on the lid so that it can be pulled off quickly to let the Jack jump up.

If you have used a cardboard box, pierce the front side and insert a brass paper clip for a fastener. Thread a cord loop through the lid so that it latches on the fastener. Leave a tassel hanging with which to unlatch the lid. Hinge the lid with tough tape.

| SUNDAY | MONDAY | TUESDAY | WEDNESDAY | THURSDAY | FRIDAY | SATURDAY |
|--------|--------|---------|-----------|----------|--------|----------|
|        |        | 1       | 2         | 3        | 4      | 5        |
| 6      | 7      | 8       | 9         | 10       | 11     | 12       |
| 13     | 14     | 15      | 16        | 17       | 18     | 19       |
| 20     | 21     | 22      | 23        | 24       | 25     | 26       |
| 27     | 28     |         |           |          |        |          |

## FEBRUARY

rain

sunshine

clouds

wind

| r |  |
|---|---|
| S |  |
| C |  |
| W |  |

### CUMULUS
Piles of grey clouds gathered together by the wind. Rain soon.

### NIMBUS
Dark clouds, heavy with rain. There might be a thunderstorm on the way.

### STRATUS
Long, wispy clouds often seen on a fine day

### CIRRUS
Fleecy clouds, white and fluffy

# A PAPER-FOLD PUPPET

You will need:

1 sheet cardboard (the back of a cereal packet will do)
1 large sheet coloured paper
gummed coloured paper squares
glue (the twist-up stick kind is ideal for this)
ruler
pencil
scissors

1   Draw a clown shape, from top of hat to bottom of jacket, as illustrated. Dimensions roughly 18 cm (7″) long, jacket 7 cm (3″) at widest point. Also draw two hands and two feet. Cut out.
2   Cut face and hands from flesh coloured gummed paper and hat, shoes and jacket, contrasting buttons and features in any colour gummed paper.
3   Cut out strips of coloured paper as follows: 4 strips 2 × 30 cm ($\frac{3}{4}$″ × 12″) for legs; 4 strips 1.5 × 30 cm ($\frac{1}{2}$″ × 12″) for arms; 2 strips 1 × 21 cm ($\frac{1}{2}$″ × 8″) for frill around hat; 2 strips 2 × 21 cm ($\frac{3}{4}$″ × 8″) for neck ruff.
4   Take two strips the same size. Place the end of one on top of the other at a right angle. Glue the two ends together. Fold the underneath strip (a) across the top strip (b) so that they are at a right angle again. Fold strip (b) across strip (a), and so on until you come to the end of the strips. Stick together, leaving the top flap free for gluing to the clown's body. Make up all strips in this way.
5   Glue the tabs of arms and legs to the back of clown's jacket. Glue feet on flat. Bend hands at the wrist and glue wrist tab to arms. Glue ruff and frill in place. Make a hole in the hat and thread thin string through. Bend arms slightly forwards at shoulders. Jiggle your puppet to make him tap dance.

Children over five can usually manage this paper fold technique if shown how. Use it to make fancy two-tone Christmas streamers.

## A FROG KITE

This design is fairly robust in order to stand up to playing with by young children. It is rather heavy for flying. If it is important to get your kite aloft, make a traditional shape using lightweight brown paper.

You will need:

1 ball of thin, strong string
4 × 45 cm (18″) lightweight sticks or lengths of split cane
a penknife
a bradawl
lightweight garden wire
green crêpe paper
red crêpe paper
white and black tissue paper
glue
ruler

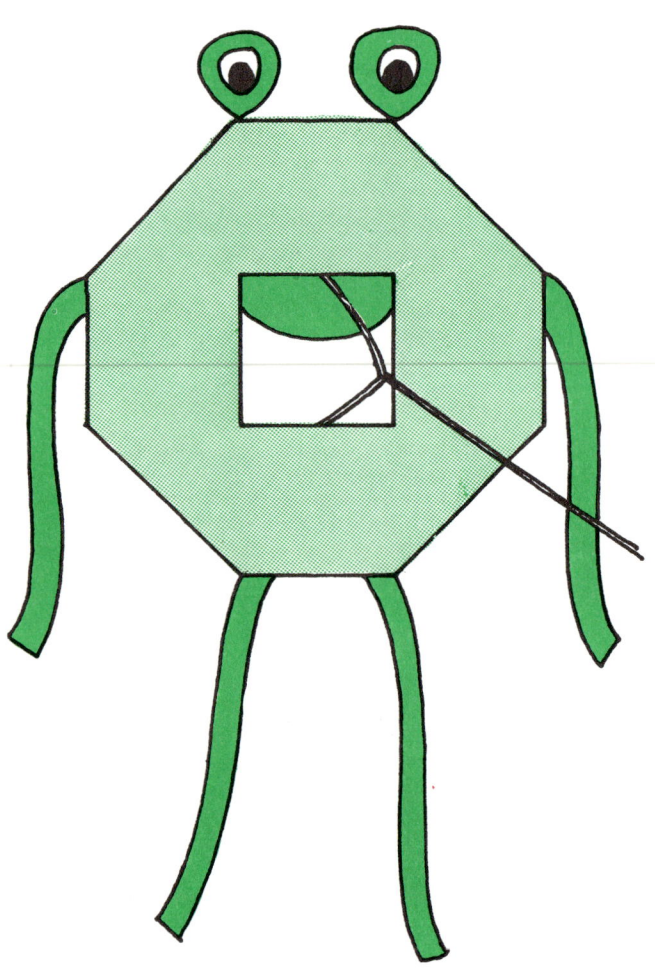

1   With string, bind sticks together as shown.
2   Cut a notch in both ends of each stick for string.

With a bradawl, pierce a hole near the end of two sticks.

3   Outline the shape by passing string through each notch. Tie tightly, keeping the string taut.
4   Take two pieces of lightweight garden wire, each about 37 cm (15″) long. Fashion each into a loop with a 3 cm (1½″) straight handle. Bind loop with pliers. Pass the straight wire through the holes in wooden struts, and bind with pliers.
5   Tie a long piece of string to the two cross-struts that are horizontal to the wire loops, as shown.
6   Cut green crêpe paper to fit your outline, including the wire loops, leaving a 2 cm (¾″) overlap all around. Cut out central square, leaving 2 cm (¾″) overlap. Glue overlap to frame.
7   Glue a red crêpe paper semi-circle to back of kite so that it shows through as a 'mouth' at the front. It should be behind the loop of string.
8   Make frog's eyes from large circles of white tissue paper, and smaller circles of black tissue paper. Glue to green paper on wire loops.
9   Glue on four green crêpe paper streamers for arms and legs. These act as the kite tail.
10   Join a ball of lightweight string to the string tied to the cross-struts. When the glue is dry your frog will be ready to play with.
11   There is an art to kite flying. Length of tail and the position in the loop where the ball of string is joined may need adjusting for the degree of wind.

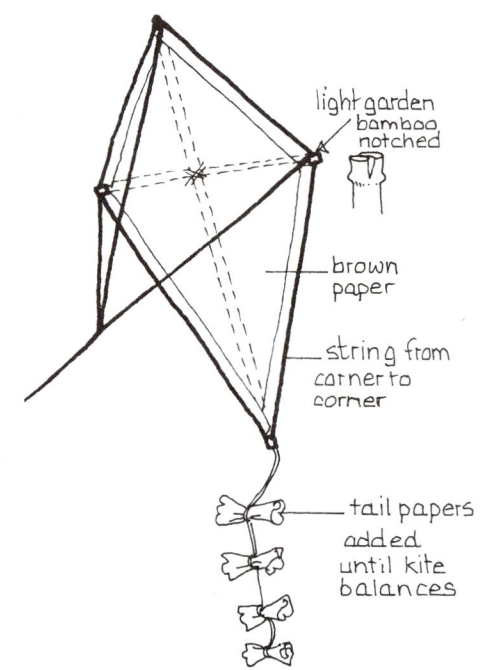

light garden
bamboo
notched

brown paper

string from corner to corner

tail papers added until kite balances

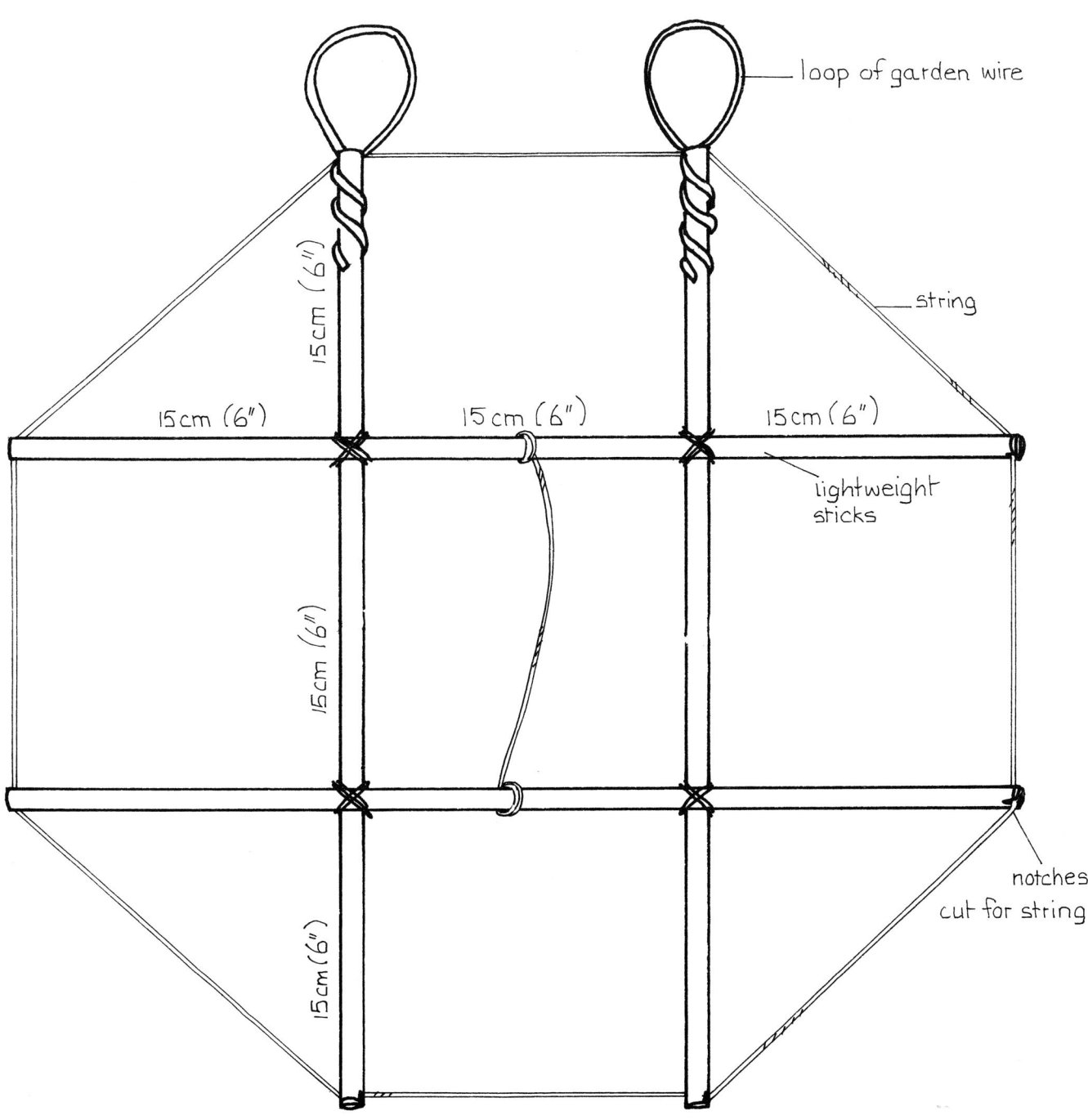

loop of garden wire

string

15cm (6")

15cm (6")

15cm (6")

15cm (6")

15cm (6")

15cm (6")

lightweight sticks

notches cut for string

113

## A FROG BEAN BAG

You will need:

paper
needle and thread
pinking shears
2 ball buttons for eyes
a packet of beans
2 circles of white felt for eyes
0.5 m (½ yd) of 90 cm (36″) wide material

1  Transfer the shapes shown to a large sheet of paper. 30 × 35 cm (12″ × 14″) is a good size for a large, floppy frog. But you can make it smaller as long as you leave a 1.5 cm (½″) seam allowance. Notch at waist, arm and leg joints to give movement.
2  The underside of the frog is cut in one piece. The top of the body is cut in two pieces, with a curving edge as shown. The curve makes each side slightly more than half of the underside. When the top seam is stitched the frog will have a nicely curved back.
3  Stitch the top and side seams on the wrong side, leaving a space for turning it inside out. Snip where necessary for movement. Reinforce corners with extra stitches. Turn right side out. Fill firmly with beans or split peas. Oversew opening. Stitch on circles of white felt and ball buttons for eyes.

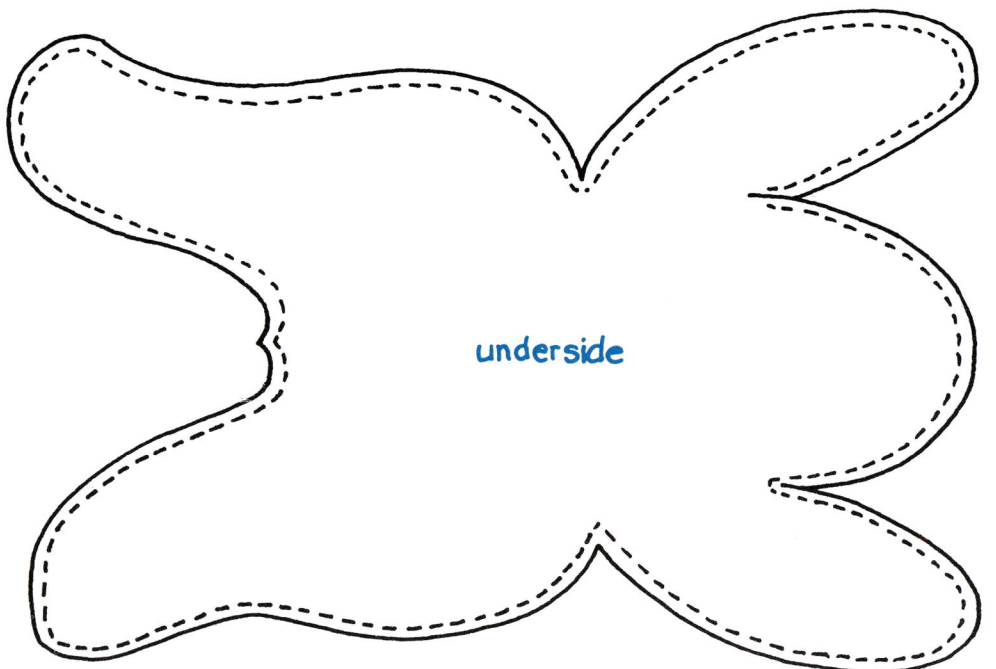

underside

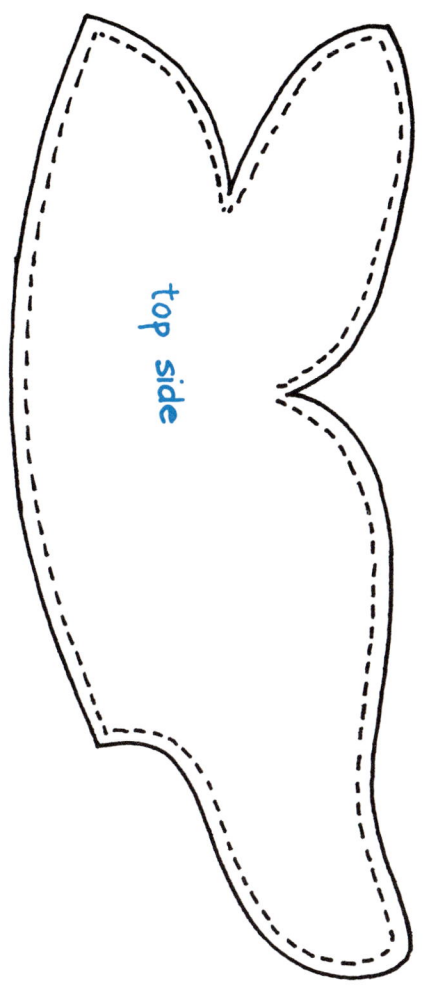

top side

## A FISHING NET

You will need:

1 wire coathanger
pliers
a rectangle of strong nylon net
needle and button thread
a sandpapered length of dowelling
piece of thin foam rubber
tough tape
garden wire
glue

1  Bend the wire coathanger into a circle. Straighten the hook with pliers.
2  Take a large rectangle of strong nylon net. Double it to make a square. Sew up two sides to make a bag.
3  Place the wire circle in the opening of the net bag. Fold over 2 cms ($\frac{3}{4}''$) of net and hem it in place on the wire frame.
4  Sandpaper a length of dowelling to remove splinters. Glue a piece of foam rubber around one end.
5  Place the straightened coat hanger hook along the foam rubber. Bind tightly in place with garden wire. The foam rubber will give it grip. Twist ends with pliers.
6  Bind again with tough tape. Wind a piece of tough tape around the other edge of the handle to give a comfortable hand grip.

## AN ARM PUPPET

You will need:

1 giant size liquid detergent container
strong scissors
flesh coloured permanent paint
yarn for hair
dress material
needle and thread
elastic

1  Cut the top off the plastic bottle. From the top opening, cut a keyhole shape out of each side, just less than half the length of the container. This is for your arm to go through.

2  Paint the bottom half of the cylinder a flesh colour. Turn it upside down and paint on a face. Glue on yarn hair.

3  Make a dress like a baby nightie, with elastic around the neck and very wide sleeves. Put it on the puppet and push your own arm through from one sleeve to the other. The keyhole shape in the plastic bottle grips your arm. Now the puppet can sit on your lap. Because it has a real hand it can scratch itself, pull your nose, catch somebody's hair, and wipe its eyes.

You can make an arm puppet as simple or as elaborate as you like. You could mould features out of papier mâché. You could make it a complete body out of a foam rubber rectangle glued around the plastic bottle base. Arm puppets should sell well if demonstrated at fund-raising fêtes.

## NEWSPAPER SUN BONNET (small size)

You will need:

½ single sheet of newspaper
stapler
scissors

1 Fold the piece of newspaper in half. Crease.
2 Fold in half again. Crease.
3 Undo last fold.
4 Cut two-thirds of the way along centre crease line of doubled sheet.
5 Cut down to bottom edge. Undo fold.
6 Staple a to b and c to d. Turn back brim like a Dutch girl's hat. Use a whole sheet of paper sideways for a larger child. You can also make it in material. Use buttons instead of staples. Starch to keep shape.

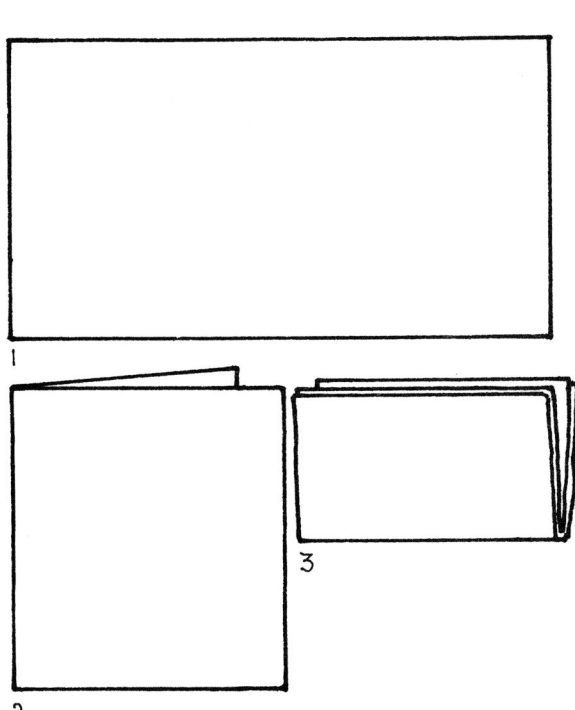

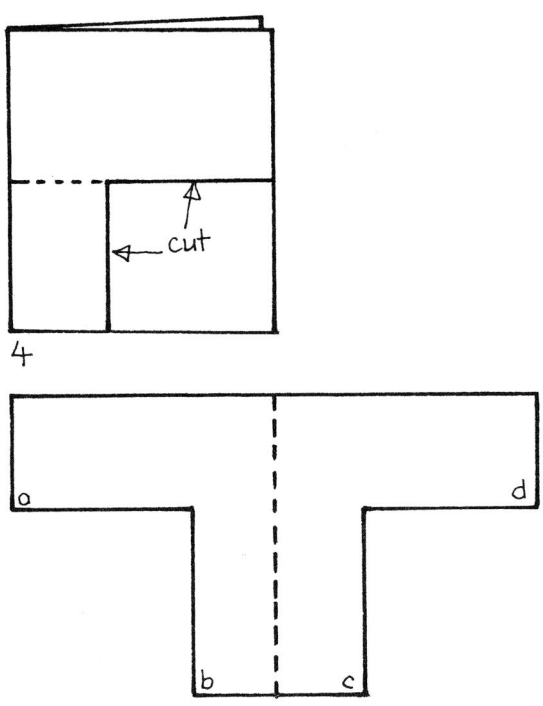

# A TEDDY DO-UP DOLL

You will need:

1 old teddy or a new one made from a pattern (McCall's pattern number U.K.59 is a good simple one that includes instructions for clothes)

2 buttons for eyes

2 felt tabs approximately 5 cm (2″) long with worked buttonholes

1 large press stud for nose

1 circle black felt approximately 2.5 cm (1″) across

1 large hook and eye as used on fur coats (available from haberdashers), or large ordinary ones if you prefer

1 hole-punch and 6 eyelets (buttonhole-stitched holes would do)

1 shoelace

2 small buckles, new, or saved from a child's outgrown shoes or old watch straps

1 metre (yard) brightly coloured binding tape for the bow around ted's neck (tape is easier to tie than slippery ribbon)

approximately .15 m ($\frac{1}{8}$ yd) of 90 cm (36″) wide felt or lightweight material for a 30.5 cm (12″) high ted's waistcoat and trousers

1 card bias binding, if you want to edge the waistcoat

Clothes and shoes can be either completely removable or sewn on teddy, leaving the opening parts as flaps.

Teddy provides practice at all the tricky fastenings that plague children when they start school . . . hooks and eyes, buttons, bows, shoelaces and buckles.

McCall's pattern U.K.59 is for a bear 30.5 cm (12″) high, but if you have a larger bear, you might like to consider using a 10 cm (4″) zip for a mouth, and adding a jacket pocket that can be sealed with a strip of Velcro.

1   Sew on buttons for eyes.

2   Sew one end of each tab to teddy's head near the nose so that buttonholes fit over eyes comfortably. Allow a bit of looseness to make it easy for the child to do up and undo buttons.

3   Sew half press stud to teddy's nose. Sew other half to black felt circle. Trim circle to suit the size of your teddy's face. Attach it with a few stitches at the top edge so that it can be undone without becoming detached and lost.

4   Measure across teddy's back from one underarm to the other. Cut out a simple waistcoat shape based on double this measurement. Cut armholes slightly larger than necessary to make it easy for a child to pull ted's arm through the holes. Sew on hook and eye at front edges.

5   Measure teddy's waist across the front, and his leg from waist to start of foot. Allow 1 cm ($\frac{1}{2}$″) all round for seams, and another 1 cm ($\frac{1}{2}$″) in width for ease of dressing. Cut out two simple trousers shapes. Sew side seams and inside leg seams. You may need two tucks at back of waist to give a good fit. Cut an opening approximately 4 cm ($1\frac{1}{2}$″) down in middle of front. Bias bind or hem waist, front opening, and legs. Punch three holes with eyelets (or buttonhole-stitch three holes) either side of front opening. Thread shoelace through and tie at waist.

6   Measure from toe to heel of foot. Allowing .6 cm ($\frac{1}{4}$″) for hem, cut out four shoe shapes in felt. Don't forget the straps, which need to be as robust as possible. For each shoe sew a pair of shapes together A–B; sew buckle on one strap and pierce holes in other.

7   Fold neck tie in half to find centre. Unfold. Stitch centre to back of neck. Tie bow in front.

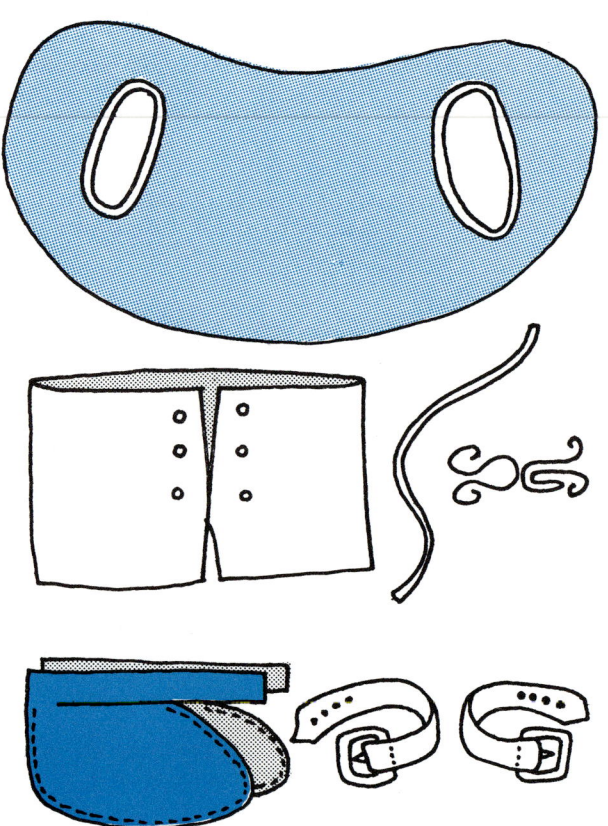

## A FELT BOARD FARM

You will need:

one 60 cm (2′) square of thick cardboard, like the side
of a large grocery carton, for a baseboard
black felt to cover and overlap the baseboard
two 30 cm (1′) squares of blue felt for sky
two 30 cm (1′) squares of green felt for grass
felt scraps
fabric glue
tracing paper, pencil, scissors

1  Fold the cardboard base in half. Unfold. Cover the inner folded surface with black felt. Glue in position, making sure that the felt 'gives' with the centre fold. (This is to make your felt board more easily portable.)

2  Look through picture books for pictures of farm animals with a clear outline. Trace them on felt scraps. Cut out. Glue on eyes and any other features needed, in contrasting felt. Cut out a big brown barn with open windows for a horse or cow to look through when inside. Cut a strip for a path, a dark blue pond with white swans, ducks and ducklings, boulders, a tree, white clouds, the sun, a nest, egg and bird to sit on a branch of a tree, a farmer.

Other themes for felt board stories are Noah's ark, nursery rhymes, and Tufty road safety stories.

You can use the felt board as a kind of puppet show, on an easel, or place it flat on a table with a box of characters for the children to make up their own stories.

## A MONKEY MONEY BOX

You will need:

2 coconuts
a knife
1 small saw
putty
glue
sandpaper
varnish

1  Pierce through the 'monkey face' holes at the end of both coconuts. Drain out any coconut milk.
2  Saw one coconut in half lengthways. Saw the other in half widthways. Take care not to damage the monkey face.

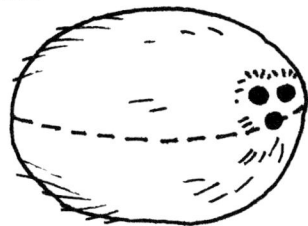

3  Cut the coconut flesh into cubes on the shell, then prise off.
4  Cut a money slot in the top half of the shell that has been cut lengthways. Make it wide enough for money to be shaken out again after it has been put in.
5  Glue the two lengthways halves together again. Sandpaper smooth.
6  With a saw, cut off the rounded top of one of the widthways coconut halves, so that it makes a base on which to balance the whole coconut. Sandpaper it smooth. (The other half is not needed.)

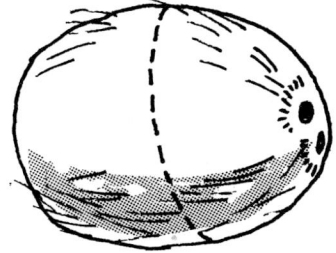

7  Balance the whole coconut on the half coconut base. Fill in any gaps with putty. Glue in position.
8  Varnish.

## A COUNTING PICTURE

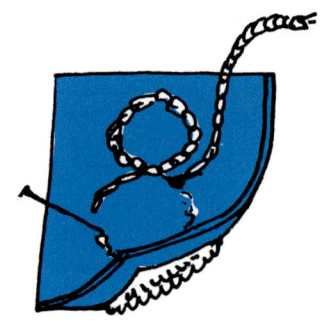

You will need:

a piece of plywood about 40 × 55 cm (15″ × 21″), or heavy duty cardboard. (Two sides of a cardboard grocery carton glued together will do.)
a piece of black felt or woollen material, about 45 × 60 cm (17″ × 23″) to allow overlap around base
scraps of different coloured felt
embroidery thread, sequins and beads for eyes, scraps of net for bee wings
glue
tailor's chalk
30 cm (12″) strip of Velcro fastening

1   Cut 2 pink felt rectangles, 4 × 2 cm (1½″ × ¾″). These are houses. Cut two red felt roofs in proportion. Embroider a door and window on each. Also cut out 1 large orange moon; 3 grey clouds; 4 orange bees with embroidered white stripes, bead and sequin eyes and net wings; 6 red ladybirds with embroidered black markings; 7 blue fish with sequin and bead eyes; 8 white birds; 10 pink flowers with glued-on orange centres.
2   With tailor's chalk rule a line about one-third of the way down your black background material. This is the horizon line. Stitch it in with white crochet cotton. With tailor's chalk, sketch in a row of nine trees. Embroider them with brown trunks and branches alternating in two shades of green. Glue all the felt pieces in position, as illustrated. With tailor's chalk, draw the ripples of the pond over the fish. Stitch in white. Draw five bullrushes. Embroider with light green stems, dark green leaves, brown tops.
3   Cut the Velcro into 10 pieces, 1 longer than the others. Glue and stitch the hook side squares onto the black background, one near each group. On the back of the furry squares, draw the numbers 1 to 10 in glue with a pin. Fashion the numbers out of white crochet thread stuck to the glue. Stick the Velcro on the appropriate groups. When your picture has been completed the children can take the numbered Velcro boxes off and work out where to put them back again.
4   Stretch the material to fit snugly over the baseboard. Glue in position. You might like to finish off the back with a piece of wallpaper and tough tape binding to discourage tiny fingers from picking the material off the baseboard.

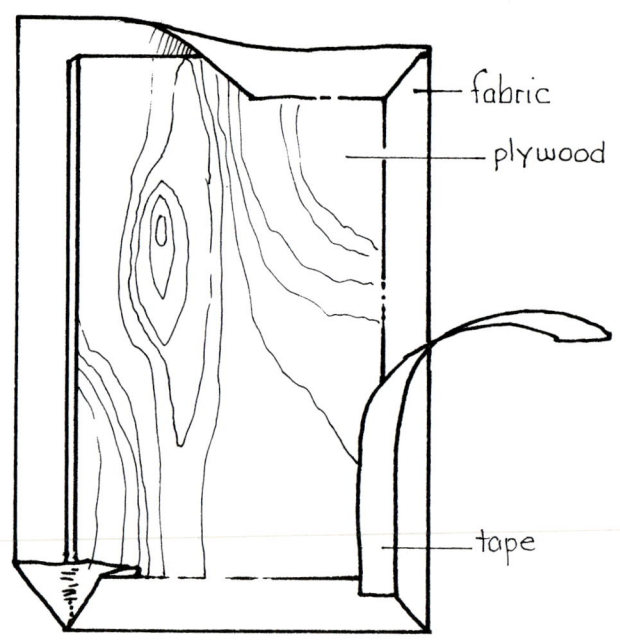

fabric
plywood
tape

# Bibliography

The following books are recommended in the text. The names of the authors and publishers will be found on the pages indicated.

## FURTHER READING

THE CHILD'S WORLD, by Phyllis Hostler (Penguin)

MOTHER'S HELP: for busy mothers and playgroup leaders, by S. Dickinson (Collins)

NOT YET FIVE, by E. Gwenda Bartram (Charles Crest & Company)

PLAY SCHOOL PLAY IDEAS, by Ruth Craft (BBC Publications)

PLAY WITH A PURPOSE: for under-sevens, by E. M. Matterson (Penguin)

THE PRE-SCHOOL YEARS, by Willem van der Eyken (Penguin Education Special)

THE PSYCHOLOGY OF PLAY, by Susanna Millar (Pelican)

WHAT TO DO WHEN THERE'S NOTHING TO DO, by the Boston Children's Medical Centre (Hutchinson)

## POEMS, RHYMES AND SONGS

AMERICAN FOLK SONGS FOR CHILDREN, by Ruth Crawford Seeger (Doubleday & Company, Inc., NY)

THE BOOK OF A THOUSAND POEMS, Collected works (Evans)

ONE, TWO, THREE, FOUR (Number rhymes and finger games), by Mary Grice (Warne)

THE OXFORD NURSERY SONG BOOK, by Percy Buck (Oxford University Press)

THE PUFFIN BOOK OF NURSERY RHYMES, by Iona and Peter Opie (Puffin)

THE PUFFIN SONG BOOK, by Leslie Woodgate (Puffin)

THIS LITTLE PUFFIN, by Elizabeth Matterson (Young Puffin)

## PRE-SCHOOL PLAYGROUPS ASSOCIATION PUBLICATIONS

40 ACTION SONGS, 40 FINGER PLAYS, by the Bath & District Branch PPA

MY KIND OF PLAYGROUP MUSIC, by Margaret Shephard (This includes an excellent list of records)

CONTACT, a monthly magazine

For a full list of PPA publications write to:

Alford House
Aveline Street
London SE11 5DJ

or

7 Royal Terrace
Glasgow
Scotland

## PICTURE REFERENCE BOOKS

WHAT TO LOOK FOR IN SPRING, WHAT TO LOOK FOR IN SUMMER, WHAT TO LOOK FOR IN AUTUMN, WHAT TO LOOK FOR IN WINTER, by E. L. Grant Watson (Ladybird Nature Books)

TREES, BRITISH WILD FLOWERS, by Brian Vesey-Fitzgerald (Ladybird Nature Books)

THE SEASHORE, by Nancy Scott (Ladybird Nature Books)

THE OXFORD BOOK OF INSECTS, THE OXFORD BOOK OF WILD FLOWERS, Oxford University Press

# Index